How to Start a

Q Place

Mary Schaller

Published by Q Place

Comments about Q Place

"I wish Q Place had been around when I was a seeker investigating spiritual issues! This is where the action is: a safe place of discussion and discovery, where open-minded people can pursue answers to satisfy their hearts and minds."

— **Lee Strobel**
Former atheist and author of *The Case for the Real Jesus*

"Q Place continues the small group Bible study ministry of Neighborhood Bible Studies (NBS), deepening and expanding outreach to adults untouched by the local church."

— **Kay Schell**
Retired co-founder of NBS and author of many NBS Bible discussion guides

"One reason why Jesus' style was effective is because he related to seekers authentically and sought to understand their questions from the inside out. Q Place offers just such a format: where seekers gather to discuss their spiritual journeys, asking questions in a safe place in which their questions are heard respectfully as they are encouraged to consider the One who can fulfill their deepest longings."

— **Rebecca Pippert**
Author of *A Heart for God* and *Out of the Salt Shaker*

"Curiosity about spirituality, God, and even religion is at a high level in our culture—but so is confusion about where to go to discuss real questions. That's why I'm so excited about Q Place! These groups provide safe settings for spiritual conversations, allowing open and honest inquiry in a spirit of respect, trust, and personal discovery."

— **Mark Mittelberg**
Author of *Choosing Your Faith*
Co-author of *The Unexpected Adventure*

"Few people are aware of the transformational power of a small group of spiritually curious folks gathering for conversation with a prepared guide. Q Place will be a catalyst for local churches and caring Christians to 'get it,' and change the way we reach our searching friends so that the average individual can experience the adventure of evangelism and life change."

— **Russ Robinson**
Small group speaker and co-author of *Building a Church of Small Groups*

"Q Place is long overdue. Christians want to learn how to talk about Jesus in normal ways and spiritual explorers want to be listened to without an agenda. Q Place enables for this conversation to take place and when people like each other, the rules change. Hooray for Q Place!"

— **Jim Henderson**
Founder of Off the Map and author of *Jim and Casper Go to Church*

"Q Place offers the perfect venue for spiritual seekers to openly discuss their biggest questions about God. It's an ideal resource for anyone who wants a safe and caring community to honestly explore faith issues."

— **Vip Patel**
Founder and president of JesusCentral.com

"Q Place is one of the most exciting outreach tools available! It offers an opportunity for people to gather in small groups and safely explore spiritual matters together. In this engaging environment people can discover the real Jesus!"

— **Nancy Grisham, PhD**
Founder of Livin' Ignited, professor and evangelism consultant

"It used to be, in the not too distant past, that spiritual explorers and seekers listened their way into faith. Today people are talking and observing their way into faith. This requires a community of people living out their faith while offering hospitality in the form of listening. Q Place is on the leading edge of God's loving response to this shift in culture."

— **Todd Hunter**
Former president of Alpha USA and author of *Christianity Beyond Belief*

"At a time when the word 'Christian' or 'evangelical' in the minds of many conjures up judgment, or the imposition of faith upon another, Q Place starts with keen respect for the one on a journey of faith. With full confidence that the journey ends with Christ, honored questions by the explorer can lead the person to discover who they have been longing for without knowing it."

— **Greg Ogden**
Author of *Transforming Discipleship* and *Discipleship Essentials*

"Q Place connects contemporary spiritual seekers to Scripture and an affirming conversational community. It is ideal both for the spiritually exploring, and for the everyday Christians who want to serve them and love them toward Jesus."

— **Dr. Rick Richardson**
Professor of Evangelism, Wheaton College
Author of *Reimagining Evangelism*

CONTENTS

FOREWORD

We are therefore Christ's ambassadors, as though God were making his appeal through us.
— 2 Corinthians 5:20

Ever since I can remember, I've been passionate about reaching out to the spiritually unconvinced. I'm not exactly sure where that came from but early on, raised in a Christian home, I somehow realized that lost people really matter. And eventually, I discovered that nothing quite compares with the joy of cheering on seekers as they take steps in their spiritual journey toward Jesus.

And so I've devoted myself to cultivating genuine friendships and initiating authentic conversations in an attempt to convey the compelling message of the gospel. I've tried my best to figure out the most effective ways of presenting the truths of the Bible with boldness, clarity and urgency while, at the same time, offering unconditional acceptance.

That's why I couldn't be more enthusiastic about this book, *How to Start a Q Place!* Recently, in an effort to remain true to its original ministry focus, Neighborhood Bible Studies has taken the bold step to ruthlessly evaluate its current evangelistic effectiveness and make adaptations and adjustments wherever needed. I'm thrilled to see this unwavering commitment to developing a relevant, cutting-edge approach to reaching out to people far from God with the gospel of Jesus Christ. And I'm honored to be affiliated with the ongoing mission of Q Place to equip Christians everywhere to facilitate life-changing discussions with spiritual seekers. This book summarizes the process of how to join them in this great adventure!

As you prayerfully read and study this guide, let your imagination run with the possibilities! Just imagine something like this: You walk over to your next-door neighbor's home and you are greeted warmly and invited inside. Within a little while, the doorbell rings several times and before you know it, a group of eleven or twelve have gathered in the living room for an hour-long, highly interactive and invigorating discussion—about spiritual matters! People are refreshingly open and honest about their own spiritual struggles and breakthroughs. They are eager to wrestle with comparing what they believe, both intellectually and emotionally, with what the Bible teaches and what others are sharing—and most of them are not even Christians!

Can you imagine such a scene? I hope so. I've been training Christians to launch and lead these types of informal, non-threatening, on-going discussions for spiritual seekers now for many years and I've seen God use this tailored approach for outreach in incredible ways. I cannot get over the impact these kinds of group interactions can make in the lives of non-Christians and how God uses this approach to reach people for himself.

Imagine yourself forming your own group specifically designed for non-Christians. Imagine identifying an ideal setting, maybe in your church, your workplace, or your neighborhood and inviting seekers to join you on a regular basis for a discussion about spiritual matters. Imagine exploring the gospel message together. When you gather together a small group filled with seekers, it's only a matter of time before you'll give them a chance to discuss it, understand it, and embrace it. Who knows, you just might experience life-changing encounters that you'll remember for the rest of your life. And when that happens—when you play a role in leading someone across the line of faith— two lives will be changed for all eternity. The one who received Christ—and yours—because you were there!

– Garry Poole, speaker and author of Seeker Small Groups

INTRODUCTION

A Simple Story

For many years I lived in a small affluent community in northern California with friends I had grown to know and love through countless conversations on the side-lines of kids' soccer games, baseball games, field trips, coffees, parties, and PTA meetings. They were neighbors, educators, coaches, or parents of my three children's friends. Most of them were not Christians.

On many occasions I had invited several of them to attend my large church in our adjacent community. The church was known for its excellent sermons by a gifted preacher, great children's programs, and a talented worship team. And yet it held no appeal for those I invited. Most of them graciously smiled and declined my invitations to church. End of discussion.

Periodically, to my surprise, one of my invitations would be accepted. Each time, I was sure that once my friend came, he or she would become a regular attendee and would learn what it meant to be a Christian. The Sunday messages were so compelling that I thought a decision for following Jesus would be made within weeks or months after that first visit. Someone would give a testimony in our worship services that confirmed the typical scenario of coming to our church and meeting Jesus there. Unfortunately, that had not been the result with those I invited. Was I a failure, or were the odds against that happening in my secular community? My friends would come once or twice and never come back. Why? I wondered. When I asked them, they said that the sermons just didn't seem to address their particular questions about God, or they felt like an outsider, or it just didn't seem relevant to their lives. These people were busy. And they were not sure it was worth investing their time to attend a worship service every week when they weren't sure there was a God worth worshiping.

I couldn't give up that easily. I had grown to love these friends and wanted them to know the same life-giving power that I had found in my faith. Occasionally I'd have a spiritual conversation with my friends over coffee or lunch. However, these were few and far between. And it seemed it was much more important to me to talk about God than it was to them. I would be so excited when we had the one conversation of the year about God that I'd usually blow it with my overwhelming enthusiasm to "download" everything they should know about Christianity in one sitting.

In late 2001, I spoke to two of my Christian friends, Kristin and Judy, about the possibility of starting a discussion group for spiritual seekers in our community. We started praying for whom to invite and when to start. I use the term "spiritual seeker" loosely. Most of the people we considered inviting would have told you at the time that they were not actively seeking anything spiritual. They were skeptics more than they were seekers. But God placed them on our hearts as potential participants in our big experiment to have ongoing spiritual conversations with our friends.

We invited thirty women to come to my house on February 26, 2002, to check out the possibility of a spiritual discussion group, which we described as a non-threatening place to have conversations about God. We suggested using the book *How Does Anyone Know God Exists?* Written by Garry Poole, this is one of seven books in the *Tough Questions* discussion guide series that is designed specifically for skeptics and spiritual seekers.

So much has happened since that first day. Each person who came back in the subsequent weeks and years has been profoundly touched by this life-changing experience, including me. I believe that God guided us through our discussions about faith-related issues, and as a result each person's understanding of him deepened. We came to genuinely love and respect one another as well. Many participants had not known what it meant to be a Christian, to admit that we are sinners who need a rescue plan. Some had thought they were Christians, but had never invited Jesus into a personal relationship, and they became true followers of his. Others who had no background at all in Christianity learned what it meant to be a follower of Jesus and decided to become Christians as a result of our discussions and the love that they received from us. God had used this group process to bring people to himself! Clearly this idea was a success.

I believe that my failure to reach my friends through inviting them to church is a common story. In retrospect I realize I had wanted to point my friends to *church* so that someone else could point them to Jesus Christ. Why? Because I didn't really know *how* to point them to Jesus without bringing them to church. I thought I had to tell them the right things about God and defend the Christian faith in order for them to believe in him. I discovered through this experiment in my living room that asking good questions, listening, and when appropriate, sharing *my* story of what Jesus has done in my life create an effective bridge to connect with people who are distant from God and disinterested in the Bible. As a result, I became passionate about helping other Christians start groups that are similar to mine. In fact, I began to envision the possibility of supporting a large movement of small groups where people in an increasingly secular culture could find a relationship with Jesus Christ.

Now I am the president of Q Place, an organization whose purpose has always been the same as the one I envisioned! This book is part of that purpose; it is designed to guide you through the process of launching a small group with spiritual seekers, a group that we call a Q Place.

A Simple Method

What is a Q Place? *A Q Place is a group of two to twelve people who get together on a regular basis with two or three initiators to discuss spiritual topics about God and the Bible.* The **Q** is for *questions*, because questions are at the heart of every Q Place. An *initiator* is a Christian who helps launch a Q Place and facilitates a healthy small group process. When Q Places start out, they are made up mostly of non-Christians who are unfamiliar with the Bible. This makes the group a safe place for them to raise questions. They feel free to self-discover what they believe by being with others who are on a similar journey of exploration. The Q Place method helps Christians go *where people are*, as Jesus did, and *be* the church among them.

The Q Place method is built on a foundation of more than fifty years of experience. In 1960, co-founders Marilyn Kunz and Catherine (Kay) Schell launched a ministry in Dobbs Ferry,

New York, called Neighborhood Bible Studies (NBS), an outreach ministry primarily to spiritually hungry people, most of them well-educated but biblically illiterate. Some attended a church. Others did not. NBS group discussions were focused on the Bible: its facts, meaning, and application. Over the last five decades, forty different NBS guides covering two-thirds of the Bible were developed, helping people discover God's message for themselves. From the beginning, the approach was to ask good questions and listen well in the context of a non-threatening small group discussion.

Neighborhood Bible Studies' small group discussions were effective not only in the U.S., with NBS groups in all fifty states, but across the world, in at least ten different countries and with one or more guides published in twenty-five different languages. In these groups, a rough estimate of a million people encountered God himself through his Word. Many of them discovered for themselves that they needed a Savior, put their trust in Jesus Christ, and then continued to grow in their relationship with him through Bible study.

In the fall of 2008, the name Neighborhood Bible Studies was changed to **Q Place**. Here's why. In the early 1960s when NBS began, most people believed that the Bible was worth studying. They were willing to try a small group where they could figure out what to believe about God, humanity, Jesus, and the church *through studying the Bible.* However, general respect for the Bible has diminished. As a result, most people in the western world aren't particularly interested in finding out what the Bible says. Nonetheless, people still have a hunger for spiritual truth. It's just that their questions are now more basic in nature, such as: "Is the Bible a reliable source of spiritual truth?" or "How do we even know God exists?" or "What difference does Jesus make in someone's life?" The new name, Q Place, reflects an approach that will engage people where they are, and over time will also open up the way for them to recognize the value of studying the Bible.

How do you start a Q Place? We would like to make it as easy as possible for ordinary Christians everywhere to launch an effective Q Place. The process of initiating a Q Place has four simple stages:

Stage 1: **Preparation**

Stage 2: **Invitation**

Stage 3: **Trial Meeting**

Stage 4: **Growth**

This book includes one chapter for each of the first three stages and two chapters for Stage 4, since it is the longest stage of a Q Place.

The process was originally described in *How to Start a Neighborhood Bible Study*, a booklet written by the NBS founders many years ago. This is an update of that booklet and incorporates changes that occurred as NBS transitioned to Q Place.

New resources that are now part of the Q Place method came through a connection with evangelist, author, and speaker Garry Poole. Garry has written a book entitled *Seeker Small Groups*[1] and has conducted workshops throughout the world based on his experience with spiritual seekers and small groups. We are grateful for his extensive work in this field. In this book, I will reference content from Garry's workshop and the *Seeker Small Groups* book. You can benefit significantly from this supplemental reading as it offers principles and stories to help you gain a more comprehensive understanding of how to facilitate small groups for spiritual seekers.

Additionally, Q Place has adopted an effective discussion series developed by Garry Poole and co-author Judson Poling. Entitled *Tough Questions*,[2] this curriculum is specifically designed to enable skeptics and seekers to begin investigating the basic questions and claims of Christianity in a small group. It is our hope that after spiritual seekers begin their investigation, they will eventually be open to studying Scripture through our Q Place Bible study guides.

The Q Place method also incorporates time-tested guidelines that encourage group ownership, such as sharing the question-asking responsibility, refraining from tangents, listening well to one another, discouraging any person (including initiators) from being the expert at the expense of self-discovery, and allowing the Bible to speak for itself. These guidelines will be discussed in Chapter 5 and are also listed in Appendix A on page 85.

In a Q Place, the discussion guide (either a Q Place *Tough Questions* or Bible study guide) will form the framework for the discussion. At first the discussion will incorporate a few selected verses from the Bible, and the group will try to discover the facts, meaning, and application of those verses together. Later, the group can decide to focus directly on an entire book or topic in the Bible. With the framework of the discussion guide's questions and the guideline of letting the Bible speak for itself, the initiator is not a leader or teacher or expert. Instead, the initiator is responsible for getting the group started and keeping it focused, as well as for building a respectful and loving community.

Most Christians are capable of doing this, especially if they are given a "road map" and know where they're headed. Granted, they will need direction, encouragement, prayer, and support. But with some basic guidance, Christians can also support, encourage, and pray for one another as they all learn principles that will equip them to become initiators.

A Simple Outreach Strategy for Your Church

How do you take the Q Place method and mobilize ordinary Christians and churches to reach out to their unchurched neighbors and friends with it? In five phases, the Q Place method can be developed into an *effective outreach strategy for your church*—a Q Place Ministry.

The last words that Jesus spoke directly to his apostles are recorded in Matthew 28 and are commonly called the Great Commission. Scholar and pastor Eugene Peterson's contemporary paraphrase of these verses is convicting:

> God authorized and commanded me to commission you: Go out and train *everyone you meet*, far and near, in this way of life, marking them by baptism in the threefold name: Father, Son, and Holy Spirit. Then instruct them in the practice of all I have commanded you. *I'll be with you as you do this, day after day after day, right up to the end of the age.*
>
> – Matthew 28:18-20
> *The Message*
> (emphasis added)

Was he commissioning all of his followers or just a select few with the gift of evangelism, to go out and "train" people in the way of life he had taught his disciples through his example? I believe he was commissioning *all* who followed Jesus at that time, and all who follow him now.

But how? This has been a perplexing question for thousands of churches over the last two thousand years. Many Christians sincerely desire to reach out to those who are not interested in coming to church. I believe that in many cases the problem is not a lack of desire, but uncertainty. Ordinary Christians are uncertain of what will be effective that they can actually do.

What if Christ-followers were not expected to have all of the answers? What if they focused mostly on listening, loving, and discussing spiritual questions that people *want* to ask? What if they could be trained in several weeks' time rather than in years of a seminary education, and the result was actually a more effective way to reach people far from God?

A church that has a Q Place Ministry casts vision for this method of outreach, and then equips, supports, and encourages Christians who realize that this is something they can do. A Q Place Ministry often starts small, even with just one person who has caught the vision and wants to spread it to others. Typically this person has helped facilitate a Q Place, has seen God's work firsthand, and has become passionate about helping other Christians learn how to start a Q Place. He or she may facilitate a Turbo Group, which is a group of people that meets for six weeks to learn the Q Place method together. A Q Place Ministry tends to grow exponentially as more Christians start groups and then keep casting vision to more Christians.

Here are the five phases that a person can follow to launch a Q Place Ministry:

Phase 1: **Build** a team of potential initiators.

Phase 2: **Learn** the Q Place method together as a team.

Phase 3: **Empower** initiators to launch Q Places.

Phase 4: **Support** and encourage one another.

Phase 5: **Sustain** the ministry.

The first letter of each of the five phases spells out a common word: BLESS. That's what happens when you start a Q Place ministry. First, potential initiators are blessed by what God does in their hearts and minds as they prepare to start a Q Place. Then, participants are blessed as they are drawn closer to God. The ultimate blessing comes when individuals actually come to know Jesus personally.

We hope that you will adopt this method and ministry to develop a practical and effective outreach strategy. Q Place as an organization is committed to supporting you with resources and encouragement as you do so.

A Simple Way to Get Started

The purpose of this book is simply to explain the Q Place method, giving you the practical tools and confidence to launch your own Q Place. Chapter 1 gives a basic explanation and exploration of Q Place concepts, and Chapters 2-6 cover all four stages in the process of starting a Q Place. There are appendices that provide Q Place Guidelines, Q Place Core Values, a sample *Tough Questions* Discussion, and a sample Bible Study Discussion. You'll also find a list of discussion guides on the Q Place Resources page at the end of the book.

There's no better way to learn about a Q Place than through firsthand experience of the self-discovery small group method. Therefore, we encourage potential initiators to come together once a week for six weeks to discover the Q Place method for themselves. This training group, called a *Turbo Group*, would meet to discuss the content of this book and to work through the discussion questions together. To help Turbo Group members keep in touch and support one another, fill out the form on page 101 and make copies for everyone.

The best way to use this book in a Turbo Group is to read the chapter narrative some time before the group meets. Alternatively, the group can read the narrative aloud at the beginning of the session. This will take away some discussion time, but there is not a lot of narrative, and group members can take turns reading paragraphs. Even if there is an experienced Q Place initiator facilitating the Turbo Group, any of the members can help the group start and end on time and keep the group on track as they go through the chapter and the questions.

The format of the Turbo Group time is simple. When you get together, always open in prayer. After this, briefly review the material or read it out loud together. Each chapter has the following format:

KEY SCRIPTURE (Bible verses relevant to the topic)

MAIN IDEA (summary of the chapter)

UNDERSTAND IT (explanation of the principles)

MARY'S STORY (a personal example of each stage)

DISCUSS IT (10-14 questions for small groups)

NEXT STEPS (ways to go deeper with the topic)

After briefly commenting on the chapter's content, begin answering the discussion questions (DISCUSS IT section). The discussion questions begin with an icebreaker. Start with the icebreaker and continue to discuss all of the questions, allowing time for everyone to share their thoughts. When you have completed all of the questions, review the section called NEXT STEPS. Determine which next steps your group will take and agree on what you need to do to prepare for the following week's discussion. Write prayer requests down in a journal or in this book, so you'll remember to pray for those needs. The prayer requests will enable you to know each other better and to support one another. Finally, close with prayer. One person can pray out loud, or the group can pray conversationally as several people pray aloud for the prayer requests. Continue this same process for six weeks. At the end of the sixth week, the NEXT STEPS will include an option that will seem much more within reach than when you began—to start a Q Place!

one WHAT IS A Q PLACE?

*W*hen *Jesus looked out over the crowds, his heart broke. So confused and aimless they were, like sheep with no shepherd. "What a huge harvest!" he said to his disciples. "How few workers! On your knees and pray for harvest hands!"*

– Matthew 9:36-38, *The Message*

THE MAIN IDEA

People who don't have a relationship with God matter to Jesus. He called them "the harvest." His heart breaks for them. They should also matter to us when we follow Jesus. In fact, he called us "the workers" for this great harvest of people he loves. Q Place is an effective way for us (the workers) to engage in spiritual conversations with those who matter to Jesus.

UNDERSTAND IT

Jesus' heart was broken by his observation of the crowds around him. He saw that they were confused and aimless, similar to sheep when there was no shepherd to guide and protect them. Like sheep, people wandered off, got into trouble, made bad choices, were attacked by predators, hurt one another, and didn't find what they needed to survive. There were so many in the crowds like that! He called it a huge harvest.

Jesus knew that people needed someone to guide and protect them. He knew there were not enough workers to shepherd those who were lost, confused, and aimless. So he asked his followers to pray fervently for more workers. Who were the workers that Jesus wanted? People who followed Jesus who could see the same thing he did: lost, confused, and aimless people looking for someone trustworthy to guide them. Jesus wanted his followers to love, guide, and care for these aimless people.

Has anything changed in the 21st century? There is still a huge harvest of people far from God and still very few workers. The newspaper every day is filled with stories of people who are lost, confused, and aimless who have gotten into trouble. You all personally know people like that. What would happen if there were enough workers in God's kingdom who genuinely cared about people far from God and could serve as guides toward Jesus, the ultimate Good Shepherd? Unchurched people are often in need of someone who will listen to them and genuinely love them through life's ups and downs.

When Jesus speaks of "lost" people in the Gospels, whom does he consider lost? The lost are people who have turned their backs on God to go their own way. So where is the harvest that Jesus describes? There are basically two variables that help us to figure out where the harvest is. The first variable addresses the question: Are they followers of Jesus or not? We'll refer to these two groups as "believers" and "unbelievers." The second variable is determined by whether they attend a church or not. We'll refer to those attending a church as "churched" and those not connected to a church as "unchurched."

Which do you think would be considered the largest "harvest" among the following four groups:

1. **Churched believers** (attend a church and believe in Jesus)

2. **Churched unbelievers** (attend a church but do not believe in Jesus)

3. **Unchurched believers** (do not attend a church but believe in Jesus)

4. **Unchurched unbelievers** (do not attend a church and do not believe in Jesus)

There are certainly many unbelievers who attend churches, but the largest harvest is found among unchurched unbelievers. While many churches are focusing efforts on attracting people to meetings and sermons, an increasingly larger group of people isn't interested in any church programs. In Mark 2:16-17 (NLT), Jesus was clear about whom he came to reach. He was asked why he spent time with tax collectors and other known sinners or "such scum," as the Pharisees labeled many of the people Jesus attracted. These shunned people were clearly outside the established religious institution. But Jesus said, "Healthy people don't need a doctor—sick people do. I have come to call sinners, not those who think they are already good enough." Time and again, Jesus modeled the principle of reaching out to people who didn't have a place in Jewish synagogues. He touched unclean lepers and healed them, cast out demons from people enslaved by them, and struck up conversations with outcasts, such as a Samaritan woman at a well.

In Jesus' earthly ministry, he also focused special, ongoing attention on the twelve whom he had deliberately chosen. Some people think that from the beginning his disciples believed Jesus was God. But that is not what the Gospels tell us. In Mark 6:52, after Jesus' followers had been with him for quite a while, witnessing many healings, miracles, and power over nature by calming a storm, it says that "their hearts were hard and they still did not believe." In this first "Q Place," Jesus' target audience was a group of unbelievers.

If unchurched unbelievers are the largest harvest (both then and now), who would be the largest group of workers? It would be those who are inside a church body and are believers in Jesus (churched believers) – those who have been equipped to do God's work in the world, outside the church doors, where the harvest is. The challenge for God's workers is this: *How* do you effectively engage in ongoing spiritual conversations with people who are unchurched and don't believe in Jesus? Are you equipped? This method may be what you need to get equipped. Then, when you're ready, consider inviting them to come to a Q Place.

What is a Q Place? *A Q Place is a group of two to twelve people who get together on a regular basis with two or three initiators to discuss spiritual topics about God and the Bible.* Q Place *participants* are people who are willing to explore spiritual topics in an ongoing small group discussion. When a group is starting, it is important that a majority of the participants are not Christians. By being in the majority, non-Christians will feel it is safer to raise questions and discover for themselves what they believe, since they are all on a similar journey of exploration.

An *initiator* is a Christian who helps launch a Q Place and facilitates a healthy small group process. This person should have a close relationship with Jesus. You can't introduce Jesus to someone else if you don't know him well yourself. Prayer and the Bible should be central in an initiator's life. Spiritual friendships with others and a heart for serving others are additional important traits. A close relationship with Jesus will enable you to have a genuine love for others because it comes from *him*.

Why is this method effective? Because it is similar to what Jesus did with his disciples. He spent time with them and informally discussed spiritual matters with them. He enabled each of his followers to discover answers about who he was at their own pace. Like Jesus, *a Q Place initiator enables participants to self-discover answers about God and the Bible.* People can learn and accept new spiritual truths at their own pace as they sense a caring, nonjudgmental community.

The initiator of the group does not serve as the expert or teacher. He or she starts the group, introduces the discussion guides, builds community, and facilitates the group process. Participants all share in leading the discussions. If a different person is the moderator or the question-asker every week, participants will sense that the group belongs to everyone and they will be more engaged in the process.

Mary's Story

I had been a Christian for thirty-four years when I first considered starting a small group for spiritual skeptics and seekers. Even though I had become a Christian at age sixteen, for the subsequent fifteen years I had not taken my faith seriously. I didn't attend church regularly, read the Bible, spend time with other Christians, or pray regularly. I barely knew what it meant to be a follower of Jesus. Twenty-five years ago I was invited to join a small group. It was there that I learned through others and studying the Bible what it meant to be a Christian. I grew in my relationship with Jesus Christ. I started spending regular time in prayer. My everyday behavior and choices slowly began to change. As time went by, I was more loving toward others, joyful, peaceful, and kind. I wanted my friends and family to experience the same thing. Eventually, I started to see those who were far from God the same way Jesus did: with a broken heart. By the time God started to "nudge" me to reach out to my neighbors and friends, I genuinely wanted them to know the source of my growing joy and peace.

DISCUSS IT

1. If you are meeting for the first time in a Turbo Group, spend some time introducing yourselves, where you live, and why you are interested in starting a Q Place.

2. Describe a situation when you lost something precious. What did you do? How did you go about finding it?

3. Why do you think Jesus' heart broke when he saw the crowds confused and aimless?

4. Jesus said there is a huge harvest, but few workers. Among your own friends and acquaintances, who could be considered part of the harvest? Who might be a worker?

5. How do you currently reach out to those who are unchurched and don't believe in Jesus?

6. Have you ever been in a small group? If so, describe the experience and how it has helped your own spiritual journey. If you haven't been in a small group, what are the barriers that have kept you from joining one?

7. If you were to identify progress in your own faith journey, which one of these four would be most descriptive of you?

_____ Exploring Christianity (You're not sure about Jesus yet; you haven't made a commitment to follow him.)

_____ New or growing believer (You believe Jesus is God and your Savior and you want to follow him, but you haven't been a Christian a long time or you haven't invested a lot of time yet in getting to know Jesus well.)

_____ Close to Jesus (You have an ongoing, consistent relationship with Jesus. You're in fellowship with other Christians. Prayer and the Bible are central to your everyday life.)

_____ Christ-centered (You love God more than anything else in your life and have given your life to serve him first and foremost by following Jesus.)

_____ Other: _____

_____

_____

8. What are your greatest apprehensions about starting a Q Place?

THE NEXT STEPS:

1. At this point I would like to:

    ____ View a 5-minute video clip of a Q Place discussion at www.QPlace.com.

    ____ Preview a *Tough Questions* discussion guide.

    ____ Preview sample Q Place Bible study guides.

    ____ Read through Q Place Guidelines and Core Values (Appendices A and B).

    ____ Spend time learning more about Q Place through the website: www.QPlace.com.

    ____ Talk to a Q Place initiator or catalyst about my questions.

2. Read Chapter 2 and be prepared to participate in the next group discussion.

3. Spend time this week studying one or all of these Scripture passages. Ask God to use these verses to help you understand what he wants you to do regarding reaching out to those who don't know him.

    ____ Matthew 9:35-38

    ____ Matthew 28:16-20

    ____ Luke 15:1-32

PREPARATION

*C*alling the Twelve to him,
he sent them out two by
two and gave them authority over
evil spirits.... They went out and
preached that people should repent.

– Mark 6:7, 12

Be wise in the way you act toward
outsiders; make the most of every
opportunity. Let your conversation
be always full of grace, seasoned
with salt, so that you may know how
to answer everyone.

– Col. 4:5-6

THE MAIN IDEA

The first stage of launching a Q Place is Preparation. *Preparation* involves four elements: understanding the state of your own heart and mind, finding another person to initiate a Q Place with you, building relationships with non-Christians, and deciding on a location for your first meeting. If you are personally ready, building relationships is the most important element of this stage, because the people most likely to become Q Place participants are people you already know. It is essential that you develop and nurture friendships with non-Christians.

UNDERSTAND IT

To be prepared to launch a Q Place, there are four main components to consider:

1. You, the initiator
2. Another initiator who can partner with you
3. Unchurched people to invite
4. A location for the first gathering

First, let's start with you, the potential initiator. Do you have a heart for those who are far from God? If not, pray that God would give you that kind of heart. Let your heart be broken by what breaks God's heart: people who are living outside of a relationship with him.

This entire process of starting and facilitating a Q Place will require attentive prayer. Jesus said he does only what the Father tells him to do. You will need to listen prayerfully and follow God's leading if you expect your efforts to bear fruit. Since Jesus says that apart from him we can bear no fruit (John 15:4-5), our relationship with Jesus is a critical part of our ability to facilitate well through his guidance.

Second, pray that God would show you someone else who wants to start a Q Place with you. In Ecclesiastes 4:9-10, it says, "Two are better than one, because they have a good return for their work: If one falls down, his friend can help him up. But pity the man who falls and has no one to help him up!" Even when Jesus needed something as simple as getting a donkey when he planned his triumphal entry into Jerusalem, he sent out two of his disciples (see Mark 11:1-7). Consider possibly having three initiators to start a Q Place, which might guarantee that two will always be there and would also make it easier to start a second Q Place if your group grows beyond twelve.

Third, pray that God would also show you friends who have questions about God. Every day you probably encounter dozens of people who are not Christians. Have you taken the time to know their names or their stories? Think of the people who are already in your everyday life. Which of them would benefit from ongoing spiritual discussions about God and the Bible? The most likely people to accept an invitation to a Q Place are those who already know and trust you.

If you find that your network of non-Christians is limited, consider some of the following ways to make new friends (revised from the original *How to Start a Neighborhood Bible Study* book[3]).

Ways to Make New Friends

- Make an effort to talk with people while riding in the elevator, working in the yard, taking a walk, etc.

- Welcome new neighbors with cookies or a simple meal.

- Join a sports team or take a fitness class to enlarge your circle of acquaintances.

- Coach a sports team or teach a class for the park district or community center.

- Host a game night or potluck for neighbors or newcomers in your community.

- Volunteer and build relationships at your child's school.

- Teach someone how to read through an ESL or literacy program.

- Volunteer at a food pantry, Big Brothers/Big Sisters, food co-op, recycling center, crisis pregnancy center, nursing home, etc.

- Join a book discussion group.

- Invite several friends or neighbors in to work on a hobby or an interest you share, such as compiling scrapbooks, woodworking, or gardening.

- Accept others' invitations to go to an event or to spend time together.

- Ask someone to help you with something. Look for opportunities to return the favor.

- Ask people about their lives, their beliefs, their stories. Think in terms of discovering who they are.

If you're spending time with people around you, learning about them, asking good questions, and listening to their opinions, you're actually getting grounded in the principles you'll need to facilitate a Q Place.

Again, our best model for building relationships is Jesus. If you look through the lens of the four Gospels, you'll learn common ways in which Jesus built trust among his followers. If you want to know the people around you, you need to spend time with them to establish common ground; to know their likes, dislikes, joys, and sorrows; to share your life with them; and to have authentic, caring relationships. They are not "projects." They are people who matter to God, just like you. Jesus hung out with his followers and knew them well. It took them a while to trust and believe him. He was patient with the process of building relationships. It will take time for you to do that too.

When you develop new friendships, you can identify yourself as a Christian in a way that is transparent, appropriate, and vulnerable. Your motivation should simply be to give your friends a glimpse of what really matters most to you. There are two simple ways to do this. One would be to offer to pray for them if they share something with you that could use prayer. Another would be to mention activities or interests related to your faith.

While you allow your faith to come naturally into conversations with other people, also look for opportunities to find out what they believe. Ask questions that encourage them to talk about their lives. As they sense your genuine and uncritical interest, they will be more ready to trust your friendship and open up even more. In Ephesians 5:15-17, the Apostle Paul tells us: "Be very careful, then, how you live — not as unwise but as wise, making the most of every opportunity, because the days are evil. Therefore do not be foolish, but understand what the Lord's will is." Ask God to help you wisely discern opportunities that could lead to a spiritual discussion. Pray that he'll give you a significant question or comment at an appropriate moment. Then listen and understand your friend's perspective.[4]

Be prepared to share the gospel message, if and when the opportunity presents itself and God prompts you to do so. Be ready, but also be sensitive to the Holy Spirit's guidance so that you know when it is appropriate to have that discussion. The Apostle Peter reminds us: "And if you are asked about your Christian hope, always be ready to explain it. But do this in a gentle and respectful way" (1 Peter 3:15-16, NLT). In addition, know your own story as it relates to your encounter and walk with Jesus. Be able to tell it simply and briefly. Be ready to answer the question, "What difference has Jesus made in your life?"

And finally, establish a location where you can host a first gathering. It could be your own home or another initiator's, but it could also be held in one of the participants' homes or in a neutral place such as a coffee shop. Ideally it should be some place convenient and familiar to those you are inviting. It should be somewhere that is conducive to group discussions: quiet, with limited or no background noise, and free from interruptions like phones or other people. Even the seating should be considered. Ideally, chairs would be comfortable and would be situated in a circle, oval, or square.

Mary's Story

I knew lots of people in our town in northern California through fourteen years of activities with our children in the local school district. In late 2001, I spoke to two of my Christian friends (Kristin and Judy) about the possibility of starting a spiritual discussion group for non-Christians in our community. I was willing to have it in my home. We started praying for whom to invite and when to start. Most of the people whom we considered inviting would have told you at the time that they were not actively seeking God. They were skeptics more than they were spiritual seekers. But God placed them on our hearts as potential participants. I wrote down at least forty names and started praying for each person on the list every day. My prayer: Is this someone that you want us to invite, Lord?

DISCUSS IT

1. Describe a time when you were well prepared for an anticipated event. How did the event turn out?

2. On a scale of one to ten, what would you say is the "readiness" of your own heart to reach out and care for unbelievers? Circle the number below that comes closest to your answer.

    1-----2------3------4-------5-------6------7------8------9-----10

    Not completely ready   Ready

    (I'm really not concerned   *(My heart breaks*
    about unbelievers)   *for unbelievers)*

3. Is there someone you already know who might be ready and interested in becoming a co-initiator of a Q Place with you? What causes you to think they are ready? What excites you about partnering with them? If no one comes to mind, describe the kind of person you'd like to find.

4. List a few people you already know who might be interested in a Q Place. What do you have in common (for example, living in the same neighborhood or working at the same place)?

5. Of all of the ways listed for ideas on how to make new friends, which ones are the most natural and appealing for you?

6. Describe a situation in which you offered to pray for someone who is not a Christian. What happened? If you have never done this, what would you say is the biggest barrier holding you back?

7. Imagine a typical interaction you might have with one of your friends. What are some questions you could ask that would show your interest in his or her life or beliefs?

8. Why do you think Jesus sent out his disciples two by two rather than one at a time?

9. The Apostle Paul says, "What counts is whether we really have been changed into new and different people" (Gal. 6:15, NLT). If you were asked by a non-Christian what difference following Jesus has made in your own life, what would you say?

10. What would be the best location for your own Q Place? Why?

11. On a scale of one to five, with one representing a score of not being prepared, and five being well-prepared, rate the following four components of your readiness to start a Q Place:

____Your own heart and mind

____A co-initiator to start a Q Place

____Friends to invite

____Location to have the first Q Place

THE NEXT STEPS:

1. Develop a list of people you already know who might benefit from ongoing spiritual discussions. Write them down below or in your journal. Begin praying daily for the people on your list, asking God to show you which ones he wants you to invite. Are there names that God wants to add?

2. While you're in conversations over the next week, practice asking questions that encourage your friends to tell more about their lives.

3. Read and meditate on the following Bible passages:

    ____ Luke 10:1-37

    ____ Matthew 10:1-42

    ____ Mark 6:6-13

4. Read Chapter 3 and be prepared to participate in the next group discussion.

INVITATION

*A*s Jesus walked along, he saw Levi son of Alphaeus sitting at the tax collector's booth. "Follow me," Jesus told him, and Levi got up and followed him.

– Mark 2:14

THE MAIN IDEA

The second stage of launching a Q Place is to invite friends. A confident and compelling invitation to people you already know, empowered by the Holy Spirit, will increase the likelihood of an acceptance to "come once and check it out."

UNDERSTAND IT

If you want to have ongoing spiritual discussions with people who are spiritual skeptics and seekers, the invitation for the first Trial Meeting must be compelling. People are busy. Why would they be inclined to come to something new and unknown? If your description of the Q Place Trial Meeting resonates with their individual needs, they will be more compelled to come. At some level they have a spiritual hunger to know God, even if it has been dormant for a long time or never fully identified. Tapping into that hunger in the invitation is crucial.

Resist the temptation to judge who will be interested when you are assembling a list of people to invite. Let God help you select the potential attendees through prayer and quiet listening to him. You might be surprised at who ends up accepting your invitation and attending that first gathering. God is the one who is going before you and softening people's hearts to accept the invitation.

Make it clear to people that they are coming to hear about the idea of a discussion group on spiritual topics about God and the Bible. In presenting the idea, emphasize some or all of these points:

1. The purpose of a Q Place is to discuss questions about God. People are respected as thinking adults and not judged. No previous knowledge about God or the Bible is necessary.

2. A Q Place is for people who would like to discover for themselves what is true about God as revealed in the Bible.

3. A Q Place is not for experts. It's for new discoveries. People who think they are experts are especially encouraged to listen and ask questions so that everyone can discover answers for themselves. Everyone is a learner.

4. The Q Place format is informal discussion, not lecture. Q Place discussion guides provide the questions for the discussion.

5. People are encouraged to share their ideas honestly and openly.

6. People learn as they express their discoveries. One person's insights sharpen another's understanding as the group discusses a topic together. Participation in the discussion increases. Interest grows. The focus is not on the leader, but on the questions (and possibly the Bible passage) being discussed.

7. It is helpful for the group to consist of people from different backgrounds who are willing to share their perspectives as the group learns together from each person.

8. Most groups meet weekly for about an hour and a half. Some groups meet for a shorter time if there is a time limitation, such as a lunch hour at work or child care constraints.

9. After the initial Trial Meeting, a group will typically meet for six to eight weeks. The group itself will decide on the topic they are most interested in discussing. When the group has completed a six- to eight-week session, they can decide whether to continue beyond that period.

The people you invite will have some fears or concerns about coming to a group like this. It's important that you understand these concerns ahead of time so you can be empathetic as you extend an invitation. The best invitations will be made in person, face to face. This way you can see how the person is responding and address any apprehensions.

Typically people are afraid of these things:

1. Exposing their ignorance

2. Being judged (an attribute that has unfortunately been associated with many Christians)

3. Being rejected

4. Being stuck in a long-term commitment

5. Not knowing what to expect

If you have built trusting relationships with those you are inviting, some of these fears will be minimized or could be discussed openly as you invite them. Ask open-ended questions to find out more about any concerns they express. Listen well to what they share and address those fears with short but clear answers. You may want to leave an invitation card with the date, time, and place of the Trial Meeting. (Look on our website, www.QPlace.com, for resources that we are making available to initiators.) Always follow up with those you have invited and ask if they will be able to make it.

Patience (remember that wonderful fruit of God's Holy Spirit?) is very important in this process. Remember that God is going before you in each invitation, preparing minds and softening hearts. Sometimes the answer will be no. If you know how to separate refusal from rejection, it will help when someone declines your invitation. He or she is saying no to your invitation (refusing to attend your group), but isn't rejecting you as a person. Maybe the first time you ask them they'll say no, but at some future date when their circumstances change, they will say yes. You may be one invitation away from their saying yes next time.

Mary's Story

Around the time when we were praying about starting a small group for spiritual seekers, the ex-Beatle George Harrison died. In several articles about him, he was quoted as saying regularly to his friends, "Everything else can wait, but the search for God can't wait." Here was a secular icon of our American culture reminding us that searching for God is important and should be a priority in our lives before it's too late.

We sent a letter to thirty of our friends with this beloved musician's quote and a proposal to come to my house on February 26th to check out the possibility of participating in a spiritual discussion group, a non-threatening place to discuss questions about God. We suggested using the book How Does Anyone Know God Exists? written by Garry Poole. It is one of seven books in the Tough Questions discussion guide series.

In retrospect, I would have asked each person face to face, rather than through a letter. However, it required more courage than I had at that moment. But I did follow up with those we invited and talked with them either by phone or in person as I saw them around town. In the weeks that led up to our first gathering I kept on praying for each person on my invitation list.

It seemed like God naturally orchestrated some encounters with the women on my list, which gave me a chance to chat with them about my invitation. For example, I went to the store to pick up some photographs I ordered. It turned out that they weren't ready, but as I was walking toward the exit, I saw Sylvia. She said she had received my invitation but wasn't sure she was interested. She wanted to know more details. I sensed God's presence in the conversation as I explained more about our plans, mentioning many of the points presented in this chapter. When we parted, she said she'd definitely come to the first meeting and check it out. And she did. Four years later, Sylvia ended up facilitating her own Tough Questions group!

DISCUSS IT

1. Describe an invitation you received that you weren't sure you wanted to accept, but ultimately you were glad you did. Why didn't you want to go initially? What made it worthwhile when you attended the event?

2. What do you think are the greatest fears of those you will be inviting to a Q Place?

3. How could you effectively address those fears?

4. Why is it important to stress the option of "trying it once" when extending the invitation to a Q Place?

5. Which of the nine points listed in this chapter do you think are most important to share with those you invite? Why?

6. How can a face-to-face invitation be more effective than an invitation by mail, e-mail, or telephone?

7. What are *your* greatest fears in inviting someone to a Q Place? Why?

8. What can you do to address your greatest fears?

9. Do you think it is important to have all the answers to spiritual seekers' questions? Why, or why not?

10. How do you think you'll invite people to the first Trial Meeting?

11. When do you think you will start a Q Place? Are you ready to set a date?

THE NEXT STEPS:

1. Find other Christians to pray with you regularly about this potential outreach. These friends may be inside or outside of the Turbo Group, and may be willing either to initiate a group with you or to support you as you launch a Q Place. Commit to pray daily for each person invited.

2. Read and meditate on these Bible passages:

    ____ Luke 6:12-16

    ____ Matthew 4:18-22

    ____ Mark 2:13-17

3. Read Chapter 4 and be prepared to participate in the next group discussion.

four TRIAL MEETING

> *W*hen Jesus had called the Twelve together, he gave them power and authority to drive out all demons and to cure diseases, and he sent them out to preach the kingdom of God and to heal the sick....When the apostles returned, they reported to Jesus what they had done.
>
> – Luke 9:1-2, 10

THE MAIN IDEA

It's time to experience a Q Place Trial Meeting. You have prepared and invited. Jesus wants to send you out with his power and authority, much like he sent out his first disciples. Until you try out the first meeting along with the participants that you invite, you (and they) may not experience the power and authority of Jesus in action. The goal of the first gathering is to give participants (and you!) a good sample of what to expect in future meetings– the experience of a non-threatening place for ongoing spiritual discussions.

UNDERSTAND IT

Imagine how the disciples felt when Jesus gave them power and authority and then sent them out to give people the message of the kingdom of God. They must have been filled with excitement and bewilderment in anticipation of the unknown adventure ahead of them. Yet I have often read this account and wondered why Jesus commanded his disciples to go to towns and villages to meet with people far from God without bringing any food, money, a traveler's bag, a walking stick, or an extra coat. That seems risky. Jesus gave a similar set of instructions to a larger group of followers in Luke 10:1-20. He didn't even want them to greet anyone on the road!

In the second commissioning there were seventy-two who were instructed to go everywhere Jesus was planning to visit. His disciples were the "advance team." These passages in Luke 9 and 10 give us great examples of the plan Jesus had for his followers: to go out and prepare people to receive him. It underscores the mission of the church: to reach the plentiful harvest.

Jesus also told them as they went that they should anticipate some difficulties in the journey. He warned them, "Go! I am sending you out like lambs among wolves." Wolves are natural enemies of sheep. The disciples were like "lambs"—defenseless and dependent on God alone. We also should expect challenges in our journey as Jesus sends us out.

Typically, as human beings, we work hard to *decrease* our vulnerability rather than to *increase* it. However, the less vulnerable we are, the less dependent we are on God. I think that Jesus placed limitations on what the disciples could take with them in order to *increase* their vulnerability. This way they would be *completely* dependent on God and not on themselves or on what they brought with them. Jesus also wanted them to focus on their task and not get distracted. They needed to be single-minded, even to the extent of not becoming involved in time-consuming greetings that would cause them to delay or miss their purpose in going out. Initiating a Q Place will work out best if we also stay focused on our task, expect challenges that will point us to God, and remain totally dependent on him for the results.

In addition to prayer and reliance on the Holy Spirit, preparation for the Trial Meeting is divided into two main components: logistics and the meeting format.

Trial Meeting Logistics

1. **Choose the location of your first meeting carefully**. Select a place that is easy to find and close to the majority

of the participants. The closer the meeting place is to them, the more likely they are to come. If your group includes mostly neighbors, consider the option of meeting in the home of someone you have invited who is already enthusiastic about this group.

2. **Plan for one initiator to facilitate and the other to host or focus on serving**. Sharing responsibilities will allow you to be more relaxed and focused, and will also set a healthy precedent of group ownership. Later you can encourage the participants to take turns hosting and asking the discussion questions. This will allow everyone to get to know each other better, affirm that the group belongs to all the participants, and encourage dynamic discussions.

3. **Make the place conducive to conversation.** Minimize distractions such as a ringing phone, background noise, or people wandering in and out. Arrange chairs so that each person can easily see and hear the others in the group. Ask everyone to turn off cell phones before you start.

4. **Have refreshments.** Beverages and a simple snack can be good companions for discussion. Make them available before, during, and even after the discussion if people have time to stay and talk.

5. **Provide sample discussion guides.** If you have a Q Place *Tough Questions* book available for participants to look at near the end of the meeting, they will be able to see the variety of questions that you could discuss. They can also see for themselves that the discussions will be straightforward about skeptical viewpoints.

   There are three basic ways that you can handle the purchase and use of discussion guides for your group. To understand these options, see page 58. If you feel that your group may already be interested in studying the Bible, consider having a Q Place Bible study guide available to look through as well. Typical first Bible study options are *Mark, Genesis, Lenten Studies, Foundations for Faith*, or *Conversations with Jesus*.

6. **Get there early to prepare and pray.** Arrive earlier than the participants to prepare for your gathering as well as to pray with your co-initiator(s). Typically, you would not pray aloud during the body of this first meeting. In later meetings you can introduce prayer in a way that the participants will appreciate.

7. **Begin and end on time.** When you invite potential participants, tell them when it will start and end. Then begin and end on time. The ideal length of the first meeting is an hour and 15 minutes or an hour and a half. Allow 45-60 minutes for the actual discussion time.

8. **Aim for the ideal group size**. The size of the group will vary from a few participants to a large number like twelve or more, but a group of six to ten is ideal for group discussion. If a group is too large, there is danger that some of the participants will dominate and that quieter people won't talk at all. If it's too small, there may not be enough diversity of opinion for a stimulating discussion.

9. **Consider options for childcare.** Babysitting is often a necessity if parents are participants. If at all possible, children should be cared for in another home to avoid distractions. It may work out better for the children to be in the same location each week, even if the group rotates meeting places. If the group can't find a sitter, parents may take turns caring for the children. Missing the group every sixth time to take a turn with childcare may be better than not coming at all.

10. **Warmly greet people when they arrive.** A warm welcome at the door or in the meeting room will affirm each person's decision to come despite possible apprehensions.

If you have carefully worked out the logistics of this meeting and intentionally prepared your own heart as well, you are ready to embark on an adventure! In the book *Seeker Small Groups*, Garry Poole calls it the "all-important first meeting." Here's what he says:

> You've established high levels of trust with your seeking friends, you've extended invitations, and people have

agreed to try out the group at least once. Everything is set. Now, what in the world will you do in the first meeting? Whatever you decide, let one thing be clear: if you invited people to come and check out your group without any obligation to ever come back, you'd better make sure their very first experience is a good one![5]

Q Place has adopted Garry's solid, time-tested format.

Trial Meeting Format[6]

Welcome *(1 minute)*
In your own words and style, welcome everyone. Thank them for coming. Tell them how long it will last and what time you'll end. Explain Q Place and your role as an initiator. (For example: "A Q Place is a place where we can discuss important spiritual questions, and my role is not to give answers, but to help us all come to conclusions based on careful thinking.")

Introductions *(10 minutes)*
If participants don't know each other, have everyone introduce themselves, sharing their name, where they live, their occupation, and their favorite hobby. Begin the process by introducing yourself, modeling how much time it should take for each person. Keep it about a minute in length. If someone in the group responds with a common point of interest, encourage dialogue among the participants to connect people to one another. But also try to keep the group on track.

Icebreaker Question #1 *(10 minutes)*
Icebreaker questions give people a chance to open up and share informally yet intentionally about themselves. The Q Place website (www.QPlace.com) has a list of icebreaker questions that you may use for this section and the next. You can print out the list of questions ahead of time and use them for two rounds of icebreaker questions.

Alternatively, you can introduce *The Complete Book of Questions*[7] as a way to get to know one another through questions. Explain that numbers between 1 and 100 are from the section "Light and Easy." Ask who would be willing to pick a number. Read the corresponding question from the book. After that person answers the question, pass him or her the book to read a question for the next one who calls out a number. Continue until all participants have had a chance to answer an icebreaker question. Feel free to follow a different plan if it feels more appropriate for your group, but passing the book and having participants read questions for each other will begin to set the tone for a group process.

Icebreaker Question #2 (10 minutes)
Try another round, with questions chosen either from the Q Place website or from *The Complete Book of Questions* in the range 101-200, called "Personal Profile." Explain that these are similar questions, but they enable participants to know a little bit more about each other. Proceed the same way as in Icebreaker #1, but this time offer the option of answering one of the previous questions rather than picking a new number. Continue until all participants have had a turn, taking less than a minute for each answer.

Tough Question for God (15 minutes)
For this transition question, be sure to give everyone permission to answer in random order, even if the icebreaker questions ended up going around the circle. Let them know they don't have to answer if they are uncomfortable. Also, ask permission to write down answers for this question, and explain that their answers will be important in deciding what kind of discussions would work well for the group. Here is the question: **"If you could ask God one question, and you knew he would answer, what would you ask him?"** Affirm people as they share answers, gently asking, **"Why did you pick that question?"**

A Brief Look at Scripture (5 minutes)
Now explain that before you end, you'd like to read a short passage from the Bible and hear their reaction to it and their thoughts on what it might mean. Select a verse that would be appropriate for your participants. Avoid verses that are too simple, too difficult, or too direct about the gospel, and choose a translation that will be easily understood. The verse or short passage should arouse curiosity and spark discussion. Here are a few you might consider: Matthew 7:7, 11:28-30; John 7:37-38, 14:27, 16:33; Acts 17:26-27. Read the passage aloud a few times and then ask for their response. Ask them to suspend their judgment about the Bible's

reliability for the moment if that is an issue for them. The purpose of this exercise is to give them a brief sample of what it might be like to study the Bible in a Q Place.

Conclusion and Wrap-Up (*10 minutes*)

1. Affirm the group's participation. Ask what impressed or surprised them about their time together. Explain that they have just sampled a Q Place discussion.

2. Explain that the group could meet several more times and dig deeper into the questions that they brought up during this meeting. Show them the Q Place *Tough Questions* discussion guide and explain that it contains 42 different questions that many people have about God and the Bible. Each question has quotes, comments, and discussion questions that help a group process their ideas about that issue. (Tailor your comments here according to which discussion guide option you think would work best for your group. See page 58 for three main options.)

3. Mention that alternatively a Q Place discussion could focus on the Bible directly since there are Q Place discussion guides that cover many books and topics in the Bible.

4. Explain that those who are interested could meet together for six to eight discussions and then evaluate how well a Q Place resonates with them. Ask what they're thinking, and if they are drawn to one kind of discussion or the other. If people are interested in discussing tough questions about God, give a suggestion for which question you might want to start with. If people are interested in studying the Bible, suggest the discussion guide that you feel would be the best starting place for your group. If the group is divided (and large enough), you can suggest two options: starting with tough questions all together or forming two separate groups. Let everyone know that they can either decide right now or think about it first before committing to more discussions.

5. Discuss what might be a good day, time, and location to meet for those who already know that they are interested. Emphasize that it would be great to meet in different homes so that everyone can get to know each other better.

6. Mention discussion guide options. If the group wants to purchase individual guides, let them know the cost (including shipping and tax).

7. Pass out slips of paper with your name, phone number, and email address, and also ask everyone who might be interested to write down their contact information for you.

After the meeting is over, thank each participant for coming. If the group decided for some reason not to meet again, suggest instead a social event like a dinner or a potluck sometime in the next six months to reconnect as a group. Don't be discouraged! People might not have been ready for a discussion group beyond one meeting. There is still growth that occurred through this process. As you talk with individuals, consider asking why they aren't able to continue. You may find that there's an obstacle that can be easily resolved.

If the group has decided to meet again, and you have followed the guidelines above, then you are prepared to officially launch your Q Place. The next chapter will provide instructions on how to proceed after the Trial Meeting.

Mary's Story

I was not sure what to expect when the morning of February 26th arrived. Although we invited thirty women, only seven or eight had confirmed that they would come. I was uncertain about the rest. So I made enough coffee for twenty-five. Judy and Kristin arrived about thirty minutes early to pray. We prayed that God would bring those people he wanted there and protect them from any distraction that would prevent them from coming. We also prayed that God would give us courage. This felt scary. We were changing the dynamics of our friendships with those who were coming. What if they thought we were weird or religious fanatics?

Ten minutes after the starting time, my house was buzzing with a dozen ladies who were enjoying the coffee and pastries. It felt natural! Two more showed up as we were encouraging them to sit down in my family room. The room was full! It was time for me to say something. I thanked them

Mary's Story *continued...*

for coming and affirmed them for their bravery in checking out the possibility of a spiritual discussion group. Then I told them that we were a little nervous too. We were afraid that they would think we had all the answers, and we didn't. But we thought it was important for people to figure out what they believed about God and we wanted to create an environment that would facilitate that process.

I told them that the purpose of this first meeting was to get to know one another and to find out if there was enough interest to start a discussion group about God. Then we asked several icebreaker questions that enabled everyone to talk. As they opened up, it was fascinating to hear a bit about each person's story. Many even shared their religious background and current beliefs. Some said they had no religious background. Others had been raised with a particular faith, but when they grew up they had abandoned it.

Most of those who came were interested in the question, "How does anyone know God exists?" And they were willing to join us for six weeks to discuss it! We figured out a regular time and date to meet. Each person gave me money to buy the Tough Questions discussion guides, and we were off and running! I thanked them for coming, and surprisingly, they thanked me for inviting them. Many of them said that they had been looking for something like this for a long time. When the last person left, Judy, Kristin, and I were thankful it had gone so well. We praised God that he had given us the courage to start and people to join us in this life-changing adventure.

DISCUSS IT

1. Using *The Complete Book of Questions* or the list of icebreaker questions available on our website (QPlace.com), practice the icebreaker question #1 exercise described in the Trial Meeting format, giving everyone in the group a turn. Discuss what happened in your group as a result of this exercise.

2. On a scale of one to ten, how difficult is it for you to be vulnerable? Why? (Circle the number below that comes closest to your answer.)

1------2------3------4------5------6------7------8------9------10

Easy to   Difficult to
be vulnerable   be vulnerable

3. Why do you think Jesus was so specific in his instructions to his disciples when he sent them out?

4. Which logistics of the Trial Meeting concern you most? Why?

5. Think of the individuals who might come to your Trial Meeting. How would you welcome them, describe a Q Place, and explain your role as an initiator?

6. If *you* could ask God one question and you knew God would answer you, what would you ask him? Why would you ask that particular question?

7. Using 1 John 4:9-10, practice the Trial Meeting section called "A Brief Look at Scripture" (see p. 50) with your discussion group. What did you learn?

8. Think of the people you have in mind to invite to a Trial Meeting. From what you know of them, are they more likely to be interested in a tough questions discussion or a Bible study discussion? What leads you to that conclusion?

9. On a scale of one to ten, how confident do you feel in facilitating a Trial Meeting? (Circle the number below that comes closest to your answer.)

    1------2------3------4------5------6------7------8------9------10

    Not very confident   Very confident

10. What do you still need to do or know in order to feel confident in facilitating a Q Place Trial Meeting?

THE NEXT STEPS:

1. Make a list of questions and concerns you have about the Trial Meeting. Schedule to meet with one member of your Turbo Group before the next meeting to discuss them.

2. This week, spend some time talking with someone whom you believe is not a Christian and ask that person, "If you could ask God one question, and you knew he would answer, what would you ask him?" Plan to share responses at the next Turbo Group meeting.

3. Read Chapter 5 and be ready to participate in the next group discussion session.

4. Spend time this week studying one or all of these Scripture passages:

____ Luke 9:1-10

____ Luke 10:1-20

____ Mark 6:6-13

GROWTH

– the second meeting

*T*hen Jesus explained: "My nourishment comes from doing the will of God, who sent me, and from finishing his work.... Wake up and look around. The fields are already ripe for harvest. The harvesters are paid good wages, and the fruit they harvest is people brought to eternal life. What joy awaits both the planter and the harvester alike."

– John 4:34-36, NLT

THE MAIN IDEA

The second meeting introduces participants to a new way of growing in their understanding of God. It may also provide the path for them to find a relationship with Jesus. The second time you gather as a Q Place begins a regular pattern of *how* you will relate to one another in the upcoming weeks and *what* you will discuss.

UNDERSTAND IT

You have effectively initiated the first session. Participants are ready and willing to return for the second meeting. Hooray, God! Jesus' words in John 4 show that we will be nourished by doing God's will and by finishing his work. Jesus also reveals that joy is awaiting us as we harvest the vast fields around us filled with those far from God. In John 4:38, Jesus tells his disciples: "I sent you to reap what you have not worked for. Others have done the hard work, and you have reaped the benefits of their labor." Likewise, Jesus has sent you. You'll be doing some planting and harvesting in a Q Place. And the "fruit" or harvest that Jesus desires is people who will be brought into a relationship with him.

There are two possible options for the second meeting: one is to begin a Q Place tough questions discussion series and the other is to begin a Q Place Bible study. We'll present both scenarios so that you're prepared for either one.

Q Place Tough Questions Discussion

Discussion Guide Options

If you decided at the end of the Trial Meeting to discuss tough questions about God, there are three ways to proceed with discussion guide purchases:

1. Most economical: Purchase only one all-in-one Q Place *Tough Questions* guide containing all forty-two of the tough questions discussions in one book. Choose the sessions that match up closest to participants' questions about God and schedule the upcoming weeks according to their corresponding questions. The book could be passed around for people to take turns as the question-asker. This gives you the most flexibility for addressing everyone's questions with the smallest investment in books.

2. Practical start-up approach if everyone wants a book: At the end of the Trial Meeting you might find that one topic hits a strong chord with all of the participants. Everyone in the group may be interested in purchasing the six-week discussion guide that deals with that one topic. For example, the topic "How Could God Allow Suffering and Evil?" comes up regularly in the first meeting because it relates so closely to our own personal experience with loss and suffering.

3. Most practical and economical for groups that meet for longer than six weeks: Everyone in the group purchases a copy of the Q Place all-in-one *Tough Questions* guide. This approach allows every participant to read through the

discussion content of any of the forty-two questions and allows the group the flexibility to discuss a wide variety of questions.

Be sure to order the books you will need from Q Place ahead of time so that they will arrive in time for your meeting. Also, make sure you have enough Q Place Guidelines Cards for everyone in your group. The Guidelines Card helps everyone understand the Q Place Basics and Discussion Tips that will help your group thrive. A Guidelines Card is sent with every book purchased from Q Place. If you're ordering only one discussion guide to share, you can purchase a pack of Guidelines Cards for your group. The guidelines and discussion tips are also found in Appendix A of this book.

Before the 2nd Meeting

Before you meet, spend time reading the "Getting Started" section at the beginning of your *Tough Questions* guide. It provides you with a basic description of the guide, the format, and some helpful discussion guidelines specifically applicable to a tough questions discussion. As an initiator, you have the option to purchase a *Tough Questions Leader's Guide*, where you can find clarification and a biblical worldview answer for all of the questions in the *Tough Questions* series. Also read the actual discussion session in preparation for your meeting.

Overview of the Tough Questions Process

The questions in the *Tough Questions* guides are designed to help people go through a ***five-phase process of discovery***. That is what makes these guides both non-threatening and effective in helping people figure out what they believe. Authors Garry Poole and Judson Poling formulated the questions with the intentional purpose of gently guiding participants through these five phases:

Phase 1: **Identification** – What do you believe?

Phase 2: **Clarification** – Why do you believe it?

Phase 3: **Exploration** – Explore alternative truth options.

Phase 4: **Evaluation** – Assess the validity of new discoveries.

Phase 5: **Decision** – Draw conclusions. What do you believe now?[8]

The questions at the beginning of each session are mostly **identification** and **clarification** questions, helping people identify what they believe and why. You might be surprised by the number of people who will tell you that they've never really vocalized what they believe about many of these topics; they have never had a venue for this kind of honest sharing about faith-related beliefs. Toward the middle of the session participants are encouraged to **explore** other beliefs. It is at this phase that they are invited to consider an approach that reflects a biblical worldview. Sometimes participants are asked to consider and discuss a few verses from the Bible itself. Then as the session comes to a close, there are a few questions that help the participants **evaluate** and **decide** what they each believe as a result of the new ideas that they explored during the discussion.

Format for Tough Questions Discussions

Welcome and Greetings
You and your co-initiator(s) should plan to arrive at least 30 minutes earlier than the participants. This will give you an opportunity to pray and get ready for your second meeting. When participants arrive, warmly greet them and allow time for them to greet and briefly visit with each other. Plan for at least a 10-minute social time prior to formally starting the session.

Icebreaker
As mentioned in the previous chapter, the Q Place website (www.QPlace.com) has a list of icebreaker questions that you can use for this section. You can print the list of questions out ahead of time and pick one that can be used. Alternatively, you can use *The Complete Book of Questions* and follow the same format as the Trial Meeting to get to know each other better and pave the way for an open discussion. Stay in the lower categories ("Light and Easy" or "Personal Profile"). You could also just pick one question that everyone could answer. Icebreakers are important in the first several meetings to help people get to know one another.

Tough Questions Discussion
1. Guidelines

   Pass out the Q Place Guidelines Cards. (The complete list of guidelines is found in Appendix A of this book.) Help everyone understand how the group works by reading through the Q Place Basics and Discussion Tips together.

2. Starting the Discussion

   If all participants have guides, pass out the discussion guides and ask everyone to turn to the beginning of the discussion you have chosen. Take turns reading by paragraphs and by questions, going around the circle.

   If your group is sharing a guide, suggest that you pass the book around the circle and read by paragraphs and by questions. Reading aloud in the group will enable everyone to have the same information and actively obtain it together, but offer the opportunity to "pass" if anyone would rather not read out loud.

3. First Question

   The first question is actually a transitional icebreaker. It will help the participants begin focusing on the topic for the day without directly identifying what they believe.

4. Facilitating the Discussion

   As the discussion unfolds, the initiator's job is to maintain a healthy group process. Depending on the size of your group and the length of time you take discussing each question, you may find it is difficult to finish a discussion in the allotted timeframe. It is important to keep the group focused and on track, but also determine in advance which questions you could skip for the sake of time. Some of the best questions and conversations unfold toward the end of the discussion. If you're having difficulty finishing all of the questions, ask the group if they want to spend more than one meeting on a single session in the guide. If they don't, you should plan in advance which questions to skip in order to get the essence of the material and still finish the chapter.

5. Scripture for Further Study

   Each discussion ends with a list of Scripture references that relate to the topic. This list is there so that participants who want to learn more about the topic will know where in the Bible to look. In your group discussions, be very sensitive to the level of receptivity your group has to the Bible. Pray for the Lord's leading, trust the Holy Spirit to open participants' hearts, and don't rush the process!

Conclusion

It is important that you end the discussion on time. In these first few meetings you are making an impression of what will happen on an ongoing basis. If the discussion times go past the promised end time, it will reduce the trust level of the participants. (If you are not trustworthy on something as simple as when you said the session would end, then you may lose credibility about deeper issues.) Thank the participants for coming, ask who would like to host the next meeting, and confirm with everyone the next date and time you will meet, as well as the question you will discuss.

Following Sessions

In the next sessions you can follow the same format for the discussion or you can ask the group if they'd like to try having just one person ask the questions that are printed in the guide. At some point in the upcoming weeks, the group may be open to a closing prayer or to sharing prayer requests. To understand the foundation and progression of prayer in a Q Place, read "Remember the Importance of Prayer" on pages 77-78.

Q Place Bible Study Discussion

If at the end of the Trial Meeting your group decided that they wanted to study the Bible, the Q Place *Mark* discussion guide is recommended as the first book to study. Mark is the shortest of the four Gospels, and you don't need background in other books of the Bible in order to understand it. The full study can be completed in four months (16 sessions). Since you suggested in the Trial Meeting that the group could try the study for six to eight weeks, plan to stop at the six- or eight-week point to evaluate how the study is going and ask if the group wants to continue. For groups that speak English as a second language or for those with limited reading skills, *The Book of Mark: The Story of Jesus* (Simplified English) is also available. Three other books to consider for new groups include:

- *Conversations with Jesus* (8 sessions): Addresses the question, "What would it be like to have a conversation with Jesus?" It allows participants to see how Jesus interacts with individuals from a variety of backgrounds: average citizens; those who are wealthy, sick, or disabled; those snubbed as sinners; and those distraught with grief.

- *Lenten Studies* (6 sessions): Examines the last days of Jesus' life on earth and his resurrection. It's an excellent starting place for participants with a liturgical church background.

- *Foundations for Faith* (9 sessions): Explores questions such as "Is there a God who can be known?" "Does God care about us?" or "What does Jesus have to do with knowing God?"

  Note: The Bible study guides differ from the *Tough Questions* guides by providing questions that are focused on Scripture for the entire discussion. The *Tough Questions* series references Scripture often, but a participant does not necessarily need to use a Bible to participate in the discussion. If participants are ready to open and study the Bible directly, the Bible study guides provide clear questions to explore its contents without an expert giving answers. The Bible is the teacher, not the initiators.

Regardless of which Bible study guide you choose, it's important that you order the books so they arrive in time for your second meeting. The first Bible study discussion will be short because it is a sample study of Mark 2:1-12, for which no advance preparation by participants is necessary. Here are the recommended tools to have on hand for your Bible study sessions:

1. A Q Place Bible study guide for each person. After the first Bible study session, participants should try to prepare for each study before you meet. If everyone prepares in advance, there will be more thoughtful discussion.

2. A Q Place Guidelines Card for each participant. A card is included with every discussion guide ordered from Q Place.

3. Bibles for each participant. For the first week, bring extra Bibles with a bookmark in Mark 2. For the subsequent weeks, everyone can bring whatever Bible he or she has to

enrich the learning experience for all participants. Reading out of several recent translations can actually provide more clarity and a richer discussion. Be prepared to lend a Bible to anyone who doesn't have one.

4. A good English dictionary. This is helpful to look up words for precise definitions.

In the Q Place Bible study guides, you'll notice that all of the questions fit into one of three categories:

Observation – What are the facts? Evidence?

Interpretation – What do the facts mean?

Application – What difference does it make?

Format for Bible Study Discussions

Welcome and Greetings
As initiators, plan to arrive at least 30 minutes before participants are scheduled to get there. This will give you an opportunity to pray and get ready for your second meeting. When participants arrive, warmly greet them and allow a little time for everyone to visit with each other.

Icebreaker
An icebreaker at the beginning of each session enables participants to know more about one another and builds community. As mentioned in the previous chapter, the Q Place website (www.QPlace.com) has a list of icebreaker questions that you can use for this section. You can print out the list of questions ahead of time and pick one that can be used. Alternatively, you can use *The Complete Book of Questions* and follow the same format as the Trial Meeting. Stay in the lower categories ("Light and Easy" or "Personal Profile"). You could also pick just one question from the book that everyone could answer. Depending on the time, you may consider doing two rounds of icebreaker questions before you transition to the sample Bible study.

Bible Study Discussion
Pass out the Q Place Guidelines Cards. (The complete list of guidelines is found in Appendix A of this book.) Help everyone understand the nature of the group by reading the Q Place

Basics together. Then explain that the Q Place Discussion Tips will enable your Bible discussions to be more effective. Read the three guidelines, adding brief explanations (in italics) that apply particularly to studying the Bible.

1. **Stick to the topic or passage under discussion.**
   Don't skip around. Build a common frame of reference. Refer to other sections only if your group has studied them together, or if they are mentioned in the discussion questions. *This will allow everyone in our group to be on a level playing field, whether we've had any experience studying the Bible before or not.*

2. **Avoid tangents.**
   Many ideas will surface during the discussion. If the subject is not dealt with in any detail in the chapter, do not let it occupy too much time. Discuss any peripheral topic after the study. *We can keep ourselves on track by asking, "Do we find the answer to that question here?"*

3. **When discussing the Bible, let it speak for itself.**
   Instead of quoting other authorities (other books, church leaders, notes in the Bible...), try to discover the facts, meaning, and application of the passage together. Avoid religious jargon and technical expressions not found in the chapter you are discussing. *For example, the terms "born again" and "saved" are not found in Mark 2, but "your sins are forgiven" is there.*

Explain that years of experience have proven these guidelines to be practical and essential. A group that follows them will be able to study the Bible well together. Everyone will learn from each other as they express their discoveries because one person's insights will sharpen another's understanding. The focus is not on a "leader," but on the Bible portion being studied. Everyone should also feel free to react openly and honestly to say, "I don't understand this," or "I don't agree with you," or "This is something I've always wondered about." No question is a dumb question. Someone else may be thinking the same thing.

As you go through the sample study together, you and your co-initiator will help the group catch on to the nature of the discussion by your example.

Pass out Bibles with bookmarks placed at Mark 2:1, so everyone can find the place easily. Explain that you're going to do a sample study together to get the idea of how it works. Take a few minutes to go over the basics of how chapters and verses are marked, that there are many books inside a Bible, and that most Bibles have a Table of Contents at the beginning so you can find a different book if it is mentioned in the study. Explain that different translations will have slightly different wording, but the meaning is the same, and it will actually be helpful to compare different translations in your discussion.

Ask for a volunteer to read aloud from Mark 2:1-12. Then begin asking the following questions and discussing them as a group:

1. Imagine you are making a video of this story. What is the setting and who are the characters? What is the opening scene and what follows? *[Note: Jesus had taught in the synagogue and healed many people during a previous visit in Capernaum (1:21-33).]*

2. What indicates Jesus' popularity at this time?

3. Why and how is Jesus' preaching interrupted? How does he react to this interruption?

4. What do you think the paralytic's friends have in mind? How does that compare with what Jesus says in verse 5?

5. How do the scribes or teachers of the law react to this statement and why? Look up "blasphemy" in a collegiate dictionary. *[Note: Under Jewish law, blasphemy was punishable by death.]*

6. In your own words, what are the scribes thinking? What is the point of the question Jesus asks in reply (verse 9)?

7. What does Jesus expect to prove to the scribes by healing the paralyzed man?

8. How does the paralytic express his faith? How do the people react to his healing?

9. To sum up briefly, what have you discovered about Jesus from this story? What impressed you the most, or what did you see for the first time?

Ask the participants how they think this session went. Distribute copies of the study guide the group had chosen and have everyone look at the first discussion. Point out how similar the questions are to the ones you had asked in moderating the discussion. (If you're studying *Mark*, you can show the identical questions in Discussion 2 of the guide.) Indicate that anyone in the group could have helped the group discover the main emphasis of the passage by asking the printed questions.

Conclusion

It is important that you end the discussion on time. In these first few meetings you are giving an impression of what will happen on an ongoing basis. Encourage everyone to prepare for the next session by reading the Bible references and answering the questions in Discussion 1. Thank the participants for coming and confirm the next date and time you will meet. If your group meets in homes, ask who would like to host the next meeting.

Following Sessions

For the next session, you or your co-initiator should be the question-asker. Model the principles found at the beginning of every Bible study discussion guide (see "When You Are the Question-Asker" in the *Mark* discussion guide). At the end of that day's discussion, ask who would like to ask the questions for the following session. At some point in the upcoming weeks, the group may be open to an opening or closing prayer and to sharing prayer requests. Refer to the section in the next chapter regarding prayer (pp. 77-78).

Mary's Story

After our first meeting, most of the people came back the following week to begin discussing the Tough Questions book How Does Anyone Know God Exists? A few even brought friends! The second meeting was the real test of our claim that we weren't there to give them answers, but to facilitate their discovery process. The last question of the first session was this: "Describe your reaction to people who are outspoken about their beliefs. What conditions cause you to dislike, or conversely, enjoy talking with them?" [9]

A woman named Marianne, my neighbor two houses away, responded by saying she didn't like it when people were outspoken about their beliefs. That was the main reason she was uncomfortable discussing faith-related issues. She expressed hope that this group was going to be a place where she could safely explore topics that were "off limits" nearly everywhere else. She said what she needed most was someone to guide her and listen to her, not forcefully tell her the "right" answers. She had gotten those in the public school growing up in another country that had an official state religion. There were still so many things she didn't understand about God.

Judy, Kristin, and I were encouraged after this first discussion session. Everyone liked the material and the non-threatening nature of our conversation. There were a few times when I was tempted to correct someone's theology when it didn't agree with mine, but I sensed that would have stifled the conversation and created barriers. However, I did have the opportunity to share my thoughts as a participant, and prayed that my life would give credibility to my answers.

DISCUSS IT

1. Why do you think Jesus asked both his followers and critics so many questions when he already knew the answers?

2. When someone shares a view different from your own about a faith-related issue, how do you typically respond? Check all that apply:

_____ I get defensive.

_____ I try to understand the other person's perspective before responding at all.

_____ I try to change his or her mind to match what I believe.

_____ I ask a question to get more clarification on what he or she believes.

_____ I walk away or change the subject.

_____ I get angry.

_____ I don't know what to say.

_____ I pray for that person and ask God to reveal his truth to him or her.

_____ Other: _____.

3. What challenges do you anticipate in facilitating a tough questions discussion? How do you think you can you overcome those challenges?

4. Each *Tough Questions* session takes participants through five phases of discovery: **Identification, Clarification, Exploration, Evaluation**, and **Decision**.[10] (See pages 59-60.)

    Which phase of discovery is reflected in the following question?

    "Suppose God did step in and wipe out every trace of evil. In light of Romans 3:23 ('All have sinned and fall short of the glory of God'), what would that do to the human population? Where would that leave you?"[11]

5. In order to experience the *Tough Questions* curriculum yourself, briefly discuss the question quoted above in #4. Now consider how a person who is not a Christian might answer this question.

6. Examine the *Tough Questions* session in Appendix C and label each question with one of these five phases. Explain why you think it is addressing that particular phase of discovery.

7. What has been your experience in studying the Bible in a small group? Has the leader been an expert/teacher of the Bible study or a facilitator of the discussion?

8. Will it be difficult or easy for you to facilitate a Q Place Bible study discussion without being "an expert"? Why?

9. How do you think the Q Place Discussion Tips improve the quality of a Bible study discussion ("Stick to the passage under discussion," "Avoid tangents," and "Let the Bible speak for itself")?

10. Each Q Place Bible study discussion question involves **Observation, Interpretation** or **Application**. Review the Bible study of Mark 2:1-12 (p. 66) and determine which questions fit into each of these three categories.

11. Consider the third Q Place discussion tip: "Let the Bible speak for itself." Why do you think this is especially important to people who are new to the Bible?

THE NEXT STEPS:

1. Decide as a Turbo Group if you would like to meet for an extra two weeks to experience a full tough questions session and Bible study discussion together.

2. Watch a DVD of a Q Place discussion of a tough question (available through Q Place). Allow an hour for viewing the DVD and then another thirty minutes to discuss your observations. What did you notice about how the facilitators interacted with the group? How did they respond to differences of opinion?

3. Review the list of names that God has placed on your mind and heart for launching a Q Place (see page 35). Has it changed since you first began praying for them? What do you think God wants you to do with what you are learning through reading this book?

4. Read Chapter 6 and be prepared to participate in the next group discussion.

GROWTH

– beyond the second meeting

*T*hen they said to the woman, *"Now we believe, not just because of what you told us, but because we have heard him ourselves. Now we know that he is indeed the Savior of the world."*

– John 4:42, NLT

THE MAIN IDEA

If you continue after the first two meetings, there will be ongoing growth for all who are involved in a Q Place. Participants will grow in their understanding of God and what they believe. They'll also grow in their relationships with everyone in the group. And you will grow in your own understanding of God as you trust him to guide you and to help you sharpen your skills as an initiator to listen, ask good questions, love others, study his Word, and model behavior that is like Jesus.

UNDERSTAND IT

The Samaritan woman had met Jesus at the well. After she realized that he could be the Messiah, she ran back to the village and told everyone about Jesus. Many people from the village came to the well to see Jesus for themselves. Jesus stayed long enough for many of them to hear his message and believe. They believed him because they encountered Jesus themselves, not because of what the woman at the well had told them. Q Place participants have the opportunity to encounter Jesus and understand for themselves who he is, much like the Samaritan villagers did. You are like the Samaritan woman who has met Jesus and wants others to discover who he is. How can you create an environment that will enable participants to encounter Jesus? And what happens when they do?

There are five topics in this chapter that will give you the basics of facilitating effective ongoing spiritual discussions in a Q Place. There are entire books written on some of these subjects, but we'll give you some highlights of things to consider as you facilitate non-threatening, effective spiritual discussions. The topics include:

1. Ask Good Questions
2. Listen Well
3. Build Caring Community
4. Remember the Importance of Prayer
5. Invite People into a Relationship with Jesus

1. Ask Good Questions

Historically, Christians have assumed they need to share the gospel by *telling* people the answers about God, the Bible, and faith. However, people are more likely to seek the truth and learn when we ask thought-provoking questions rather than just give answers. In fact, God set the precedent himself all through the Bible in his interactions with people. In the first recorded dialogue that God had with Adam and Eve in Genesis 3, God asked them a string of four questions: *Where are you? Who told you that you were naked? Have you eaten the fruit that I commanded you not to eat from? What is this you have done?*

I can't help but wonder why God asked questions in his interaction with Adam and Eve. He already knew the answers! God knew they were hiding because they were naked and ashamed. He knew Adam would blame Eve for the disobedient act. God knew that Eve would blame the serpent. Yet, God asked the questions. Why? Jesus asked both his followers and critics many questions too. In Mark 8 alone, he asked sixteen questions! What was their purpose?

I think that questions challenge us to think, to choose, to respond with freedom. Questions invite us into discovery and dialogue, while answers often shut down dialogue and divide us. In Mark 8 Jesus kept the dialogue alive by asking his disciples and the Pharisees questions such as, *Why do you people keep demanding a miraculous sign? Why are you so worried about having no food? Won't you ever learn or understand? Who do people say I am? Who do you say I am?* Jesus wanted people to discover for themselves what was true. Oftentimes, a question is the best way to express love and respect.

There's an old proverb that says, "Tell me and I'll forget, show me and I'll remember, involve me and I'll understand." When people are told something, it doesn't have nearly the impact that occurs when they discover it themselves through their own involvement. Powerful questions initiate community, creating accountability and commitment. Questions are an essential tool of engagement in a Q Place. When possible, use open-ended questions that require more than a "yes," "no," or short answer. Great questions that encourage learning often begin with "how," "what," or "why."

Three basic questions can apply to almost any faith-related discussion:

1. **What do you mean by that?** (enables you to gain information)

2. **How did you come to that conclusion?** (reveals reasons for someone's belief or degree of understanding)

3. **Can you help me understand this?** (this clarifying question may help the person recognize the weakness in an unsupported claim or belief)

By using these questions strategically, you can respectfully show that you aren't in agreement with the participant's belief without getting into a debate or giving answers before participants are ready for them. They're useful to help participants work through their own thinking.

2. Listen Well

Listening is a fundamental part of a Q Place. If you are effective in asking questions, listening becomes the most consistent way to communicate that you care and want to understand. It builds trust and acceptance. You model good listening for others when you are a good listener. It is respectful. I also think that's why God gave us two ears and only one mouth: so we would be inclined to listen more than we speak!

In *Seeker Small Groups*, Garry Poole shows how effective it is to listen before trying to communicate the gospel. In fact, his book and workshops rest on the principles of *empathic evangelism*, which he defines as: *The process of guiding non-Christians to self-discover biblical truths by seeking first to understand through asking great questions and listening really well.*

There have been many good articles and books written on listening. Garry references Steven Covey's book *The Seven Habits of Highly Effective People* when he identifies five levels of listening: (1)ignoring, (2)pretending, (3)selective listening, (4)attentive listening, and (5)empathic listening. This last level of listening is described by Covey as "seeking first to understand, then to be understood."[12] Do not miss reading the chapter entitled "Listen Well"[13] in Garry's *Seeker Small Groups* book. It is very helpful. Practice your listening skills. Ask for feedback from people who will be honest with you. This is important to get right! Empathic listening will lead to great discussions. Anything less than that will slow them down.

3. Build Caring Community

The most important ingredient in any Q Place is love. It is compelling. People are drawn to places where love is shown and experienced. To be loved and accepted is the universal longing of the human heart. When you invite people to belong to a small group community and give them freedom to accept or reject God, these are expressions of God's love. Asking good questions and empathic listening are ways to show love. In Paul's first letter to the Corinthians, he writes, "Knowledge puffs up, but love builds up" (1 Cor. 8:1b).

The Apostle John said:

> Dear friends, let us love one another, for love comes from God. Everyone who loves has been born of God and knows God. Whoever does not love does not know God,

because God is love. This is how God showed his love among us: He sent his one and only Son into the world that we might live through him. This is love: not that we loved God, but that he loved us and sent his Son as an atoning sacrifice for our sins. Dear friends, since God so loved us, we also ought to love one another. No one has ever seen God; but if we love one another, God lives in us and his love is made complete in us.

— 1 John 4:7-12

Enabled by the power of the Holy Spirit, you are building a community that is rooted in love. In addition to the regular Q Place meetings, there are many ways to express love and build a caring community. Here are just a few ideas:

1. Periodically have lunch together in someone's home or in a restaurant.

2. Keep track of birthdays and celebrate them, or celebrate common national or Christian holidays when appropriate.

3. Have an "open chair." Encourage participants to keep the group open to others and bring friends.

4. When someone is in crisis, encourage others to support that person through meals, prayers, and practical help, such as assisting with household tasks.

5. Find service projects that you can do together to help others outside the group.

6. Meet periodically with individuals from your Q Place to get to know them better on a one-on-one basis.

4. Remember the Importance of Prayer

Prayer is the foundational building block of any Q Place. From the beginning, prayer is needed to start a Q Place and it will continue to be a necessary component of any effective Q Place, because this is God's work. God is in the business of changing minds and hearts, not you.

In the beginning, prayer will not be visible to participants. It's something that happens "behind the scenes." You should pray *before* the participants arrive, *after* they leave, and during the days between your meetings. At some point in time, when you sense it is appropriate, indicate to the participants that you and your co-initiators are willing to pray for them as they are willing to share prayer requests. You could keep a prayer journal in which someone from the group writes down requests.

Toward the end of the meeting, before you conclude, you could ask the group if there are things about which they'd like prayer. Assure them that what they share is confidential. After prayer requests are shared, one of the initiators could briefly close in prayer, covering those requests. If you're doing a Q Place Bible study, there will be another way to involve the group in prayer. With the exception of the *Mark* study guide, at the end of each Bible study discussion there is a prayer that summarizes the key points. You can ask the group if they'd like to read the prayer together as a way of closing the discussion. There are more ideas for group prayer available on our website, www.QPlace.com, in a resource called "Praying Together."

5. Invite People into a Relationship with Jesus

There will come a time for many participants in which they are ready to make a decision to follow Jesus and invite him into their life. In my experience, this happens more often outside the group setting. When someone expresses interest in wanting a personal relationship with Jesus, what do you do? Find a quiet place to pray with them. Indicate that it's as simple as ABC:

- **A**dmit that you are a sinner

- **B**elieve that Jesus died for your sins and that as God he forgives you

- **C**ommit to following him

Encourage them to pray with you, using their own words. Ask them if at some point they would be willing to share this decision with the group. When a participant shares what it was like to cross the line of faith, everyone else in the group will be able to see a new story of God's work in a person's life, and may also begin to consider more personal questions about Jesus for themselves.

Mary's Story

As time went on in our group, Marianne found that it really was a safe place to explore spiritual topics. Marianne had many questions. But I knew she wasn't ready to hear my answers. She came every week. Sometimes, when the group would discuss a question, I wouldn't give an answer at all. Then, she would say to me, "Mary you didn't answer the question. What do you think?" When anyone in the group specifically asked me to answer a question, I sensed that they really wanted to know what I thought. I didn't have to be outspoken or forceful, because they were ready to hear what I had to say. I had tried to listen well to Marianne and the others in the group.

Marianne became our regular baker; she made the most amazing Danish desserts! She would re-arrange her entire weekly schedule to make sure she could attend our group and bring treats. We often met at her house. Eventually she and her husband started attending a local church. I saw a lot of spiritual growth in Marianne!

There was another woman named Denise who came every week as well. She was an attorney who worked part-time and also arranged her work schedule around our group meetings. After several months of participating in our group and discussing a few of the Tough Questions guides, Denise came up to me after one of our gatherings. In the process of answering one of the questions that session, I had the opportunity to briefly share with the group that I had a personal relationship with Jesus Christ. Another participant had also recently shared with the group that she had just made a decision to become a Christian.

These comments were on Denise's mind, and she told me that she didn't think she had a personal relationship with Jesus, though she had gone to church all of her life. She wanted God to be more personal and relevant to her life. How could she do that? I told her that it was as simple as ABC: admit that she was a sinner; believe that Jesus died for her sins as the Son of God, and commit to following

Jesus. We sat down in my living room and Denise prayed to invite Jesus into her life. Five years later, after studying the Bible and growing in her faith, Denise was thinking of leading her own Tough Questions group!

DISCUSS IT

1. Who is the best listener you know personally? What makes him or her a good listener?

2. Why do you think Christians assume they need to share the gospel by *telling* people the answers about God and the Bible?

3. Steven Covey identifies five levels of listening. On which level do you think that you most often listen to others?

   _____ Ignoring what is being said

   _____ Pretending to listen

   _____ Selective listening

   _____ Attentive listening

   _____ Empathic listening

4. How do you think you could improve your listening skills?

5. Describe a group of people (family or friends) with whom you feel loved and accepted. What do you think created that sense of love, belonging, and acceptance?

6. On a scale of one to ten, how confident are you praying in a group or with another person? How could you increase your confidence? (Circle the number below that comes closest to your answer.)

1------2------3------4------5------6------7------8------9------10

Not confident   Very confident

7. Describe someone you know personally whose behavior provides the strongest evidence or witness that Christianity is true.

8. What would others say about your life as evidence for why Christianity is true?

9. Jesus describes "fruit" in John 4:36 as "people brought to eternal life." Have you ever had the experience of seeing Jesus produce this kind of fruit through your own life? If so, share one example. If not, what will it take to be ready to invite someone into a personal relationship with Jesus?

10. What have you enjoyed most about this Turbo Group? What is your biggest take-away from the discussions?

11. What questions do you still have about starting a Q Place?

12. Would you like to continue meeting with this group as you start to initiate your own Q Place? If so, how often?

13. On a scale of one to ten, how likely are you to start your own Q Place? Explain. (Circle the number below that comes closest to your answer.)

1------2------3------4------5------6------7------8------9------10

Not very likely   I am going
to start one   to start one

THE NEXT STEPS:

1. Pray for God's leading to help you know your next step.

2. Decide if you will continue to meet with your Q Place Turbo Group on a regular basis.

3. Consider options for forming a triad with other initiators so that you can disciple one another as you facilitate or get ready to facilitate a Q Place.

4. Start a Q Place.

Appendix A

Q Place Guidelines

Q Place Basics

1. The purpose of a Q Place is to discuss questions about God.

2. An initiator starts a Q Place and facilitates a healthy small group process.

3. Q Place is not for experts. It's for new discoveries. If you think you are an expert, resist the urge to teach. Instead, try to listen and ask questions so that everyone can discover answers for themselves.

4. The format is informal discussion, not lecture. Q Place discussion guides provide the questions for the discussion.

5. Share your ideas honestly and openly.

6. At each session a different person can ask the questions and moderate; rotating the question-asking encourages group ownership and dynamic discussions. Answers are directed to the group, and the moderator should not put a stamp of approval or disapproval on answers.

7. Maintain confidentiality, courtesy, and respect toward others, even if they don't agree with your position. Do not judge others and avoid side conversations.

8. Do not attempt to resolve all differences or conflicts of opinion. Keep moving when there seems to be an impasse.

9. If at all possible, read the chapter and answer the questions ahead of time.

10. Begin and end on time.

11. Review the Q Place guidelines whenever there's a new person in the group.

Q Place Guidelines
(continued)

Q Place Discussion Tips

1. **Stick to the topic or passage under discussion.**

    Don't skip around. Build a common frame of reference. Refer to other sections only if your group has studied them together, or if they are mentioned in the discussion questions.

2. **Avoid tangents.**

    Many ideas will surface during the discussion. If the subject is not dealt with in any detail in the chapter, do not let it occupy too much time. Discuss any peripheral topic after the study.

3. **When discussing the Bible, let it speak for itself.**

    Instead of quoting other authorities (other books, church leaders, notes in the Bible...), try to discover the facts, meaning, and application of the passage together. Avoid religious jargon and technical expressions not found in the chapter you are discussing.

Appendix B

Q Place Core Values

Self-Discovery
People grow and learn best
when they discover truth for themselves
through discussion and study.

Safe Place
An ideal environment for spiritual growth
is in a small group
where personal dignity is valued
and leadership is shared.

Spirit
God's Spirit will guide those
who are spiritually open.

Scripture
The Bible and the life of Jesus
are worth serious examination.

Appendix C

Sample *Tough Questions* Discussion[14]

Where Did Evil Come From?

OPEN FOR DISCUSSION

1. Describe a recent encounter you've had with some form of evil, which prompted you to wonder why this kind of thing ever happens.

2. Who or what did you blame for the wrong that occurred in the situation you described above? Give reasons for your response. How did those around you see the situation?

STRAIGHT TALK

Philosophers have categorized two kinds of evil:

Moral evil — man's own inhumanity to man, based on hate, greed, or overindulgence

Natural evil – evils brought on by natural causes in the world, such as floods, earthquakes, or tornadoes and different sorts of diseases, accidents, and injuries

3. Using your previous example, would you categorize that evil you experienced as moral evil, natural evil, or a combination of the two? Why? Does the category or type of evil influence how you determine where to place the blame for evil?

4. Take your best shot at briefly explaining why we live in a world filled with so much evil and suffering.

Unable or Unwilling?

Doesn't it make sense that God, by default, is the author of evil if he created everything else? This progression of thought usually brings people full circle, back to wondering what kind of God exists – or even if he does exist.

David Hume, the eighteenth-century Scottish skeptic, put it this way: "Is he willing to prevent evil, but not able? Then he is impotent. Is he able, but not willing? Then he is malevolent. Is he both able and willing? Whence then is evil?"

5. Summarized below are two conclusions based on the above observations. Defend or refute the logic behind each.

Because we live in a world where evil does exist,

- God must not really exist after all; otherwise he would not have created such a place filled with evil.

- God might still exist, but not in the way the Bible depicts him (as all-powerful and loving); otherwise he would have had both the ability and the desire to create a world without so much evil.

The Free-Choice Risk

Here is a very different argument addressing the problem of evil.

1. God created the universe without evil and suffering.

2. God created perfect human beings.

3. God created humans with a complete ability to freely choose between staying in harmony with God or rejecting him.

4. Humankind freely chose to turn away from God.

5. Evil and suffering entered the world as a result of that separation from God.

Norman Geisler describes the above reasoning this way: We have a real choice about what we do. God made us that way so we could be like him and could love freely (forced love is not love at all, is it?). But in making us that way, he also allowed for the possibility of evil. To be free we had to have not only the opportunity to choose good, but also the ability to choose evil. That was the risk God knowingly took. That doesn't make him responsible for evil. He created the *fact* of freedom; we perform the *acts* of freedom. He [God] made evil *possible*; men made evil *actual*.

Cliffe Knechtle states in his book *Give Me an Answer*, "Genesis 1 clearly communicates that when God created, all his creation was very good. God did not create evil, suffering or death. He created us to enjoy himself, each other and to celebrate his gift of life. Genesis 3 is the tragic record of how man and woman chose to reject God. The Bible, history books and the morning newspaper record how an immeasurable amount of evil has followed in the wake of human rebellion against God. The vast majority of this carnage is a direct result of human choice."[15]

6. The above explanation introduces the element of a free choice by humankind to reject or accept God — with resulting consequences. Given the magnitude of the risk, what value do you suppose God placed on granting people freedom of choice (according to this perspective)?

7. How would you explain the correlation between separation from God and the entrance of evil and suffering into the world?

8. Share your opinion of the following statement:

   "God cannot both create human beings with a total ability to freely make meaningful choices and at the same time control them so they always choose good."

HEART OF THE MATTER

9. Do you consider your freedom of choice to be a gift from God? Why or why not? What would human relationships be like without free will?

10. If you could eliminate all evil, suffering, and sin (wrongdoing) in your life by giving up your free will, would you do it? Explain.

11. Do you ever become angry at God for the things that go wrong in your life? Why or why not?

12. Check the statement(s) below that best describes your position at this point. Share your selection with the rest of the group and give reasons for your response.

____I believe that the origin of evil is ultimately God's responsibility.

____I'm convinced that evil is the result of humankind's rejection of God.

____Evil is a misnomer; the universe operates without a moral component.

____I'm fairly certain that our freedom to choose is a gift from God.

____I'm convinced that our freedom to choose has nothing to do with God.

____I find myself blaming God for things that go wrong in my life.

____I find myself blaming myself for things that go wrong in my life.

____Write your own brief phrase here: _____
_____
_____

Note: In addition to the content represented in this appendix, every Tough Questions *discussion includes an introduction that sets up the discussion, quotes from skeptics, quotes from Christian apologists, and a list of Scriptures for further reference.*

Appendix D

Sample Bible Study Discussion[16]

(See page 66 for the Bible Study of Mark 2:1-12, the sample that is recommended for use in a Q Place that is just getting started.)

Mark 1 – Jesus' Early Ministry

During the events of Mark's Gospel, Roman legions are keeping the peace in an empire that extends from Britain in the west to Persia in the east. John the Baptist and Jesus begin their ministries in Galilee and along the Jordan River, unnoticed by Tiberius Caesar in Rome and his governors in Palestine.

Verse 1 can be read as the title for the whole book of Mark. **Christ** is a title, the Greek word for **Messiah**, meaning anointed.

Read Mark 1:1-8

1. Mark quotes Old Testament prophecy about a messenger who will come from God. Where will the messenger work?

   What is his task?

   What is his message?

2. In what ways does John the baptizer fulfill the Old Testament prophecy about the messenger?

Note: To the Jews, John's dress signified he was a prophet like the Old Testament prophet Elijah. His food was that of the poor.

3. In what ways would John's ministry prepare the people for the Messiah?

   How does repentance prepare us to receive a Savior?

Read Mark 1:9-15

4. Locate Galilee, Nazareth, Jerusalem, and the Jordan River on the map on page 118. Notice that Jesus walks more than 60 miles to be baptized by John. What are the unique events at Jesus' baptism?

   How are the Father, the Son, and the Holy Spirit represented here?

5. Imagine verses 12 and 13 as a large painting. What facts about the temptation does Mark emphasize by the setting, and who and what he includes?

6. After his temptation, Jesus begins to preach the good news of God in Galilee. What does this suggest about the outcome of his temptation?

7. What similarities and what differences do you see between Jesus' preaching (verse 15) and John's (verses 4, 7, 8)?

Read Mark 1:16-20

8. From what class of society does Jesus call his first disciples? Why, do you think, does he not call religious leaders, scribes, and priests?

9. How does Jesus change the focus of the work of Simon and Andrew?

   What indications are there that James and John are perhaps younger and financially better off than Simon and Andrew?

10. What comments might the families or neighbors have made when these four followed Jesus?

What reactions would there be today?

Read Mark 1:21-28

11. In the synagogue at Capernaum, what impresses the people about Jesus' teaching (verses 22, 27)?

12. How does the unclean spirit address and identify Jesus?

What pronoun does the spirit use in referring to himself?

What does he fear?

13. How do Jesus' two commands make it clear that he regards the unclean spirit as a separate entity from the man it is possessing?

Note: Do not spend a lot of time at this point discussing evil spirits. Mark will mention them several times in his book and you will learn more as you study further.

Read Mark 1:29-34

14. How do the four disciples react to the crisis they find in the home of Simon and Andrew?

15. What events of this Sabbath day stimulate the crowd's activity at sundown?

Note: The Jewish Sabbath ends at sundown.

16. Once again Jesus refuses to let demons speak (verses 25, 34). What reasons do you think he has for this action?

Read Mark 1:35-39

17. On the Sabbath day Jesus taught in the synagogue, cast out the evil spirit, healed Simon's mother-in-law, and after sunset healed the sick and cast out many demons from the people the crowd brought. After such a day, when, where and why does Jesus pray?

18. Why are Simon and the disciples looking for Jesus?

How is this a temptation for Jesus?

19. Why does Jesus set the priorities on his ministry of preaching and healing as he does?

Locate on your map the places where Jesus preaches in his early ministry.

Read Mark 1:40-45

20. The reader might conclude from verse 38 that Jesus does not care about people's physical needs, but in verse 40, Mark records Jesus' response to a man with leprosy. What question does the man have?

21. What would it mean to this man to have Jesus touch him rather than just speak to him?

22. How does the man's disobedience to Jesus' strict order interfere with Jesus' plan?

Note: The term "leprosy" included some other skin diseases as well as leprosy itself. Under Jewish law anyone who recovered from such a skin disease had to be examined by a priest and go through a ceremony of restoration (Leviticus 14). After receiving a certificate that he was clean, he could return to live in society.

SUMMARY

1. How does Mark begin to prove his thesis that Jesus is the Christ, the Son of God?

2. What indications are there that Jesus is also truly human?

3. What impressions do you have of Jesus thus far?

CONCLUSION

Mark begins his record of the life of Jesus Christ with Jesus' public ministry rather than with his birth as Matthew and Luke do. Mark links Jesus to the Old Testament prophecies of the Messiah by including the purpose and effect of John the Baptist's ministry. He begins to reveal who Jesus is by describing Jesus' baptism, temptation, and early preaching and healing ministry in Galilee.

NOTES

1. Garry Poole, *Seeker Small Groups* (Grand Rapids, MI: Zondervan, 2003).

2. Garry Poole and Judson Poling, *Tough Questions* Series (Grand Rapids, MI: Zondervan, 2003). The series consists of: *How Does Anyone Know God Exists? What Difference Does Jesus Make? How Reliable Is the Bible? How Could God Allow Suffering and Evil? Don't All Religions Lead to God? Do Science and the Bible Conflict? Why Become a Christian?* and the *Tough Questions Leader's Guide*.

3. Marilyn Kunz and Catherine Schell, *How to Start a Neighborhood Bible Study* (Dobbs Ferry, NY: NBS Publishers, 2000), 35.

4. For more in-depth coverage of these ideas, consider studying Garry Poole's *The Three Habits of Highly Contagious Christians* (Grand Rapids, MI: Zondervan, 2003) in a small group discussion setting.

5. Seeker Small Groups, 100-101.

6. Ibid, 102-109.

7. Garry Poole, *The Complete Book of Questions* (Grand Rapids, MI: Zondervan, 2003).

8. *Seeker Small Groups*, 38-41.

9. Garry Poole, *How Does Anyone Know God Exists?* (Grand Rapids: Zondervan, 1998), 16.

10. *Seeker Small Groups*, 38-41.

11. This question comes from the *How Could God Allow Suffering and Evil?* topic, under the question "Why Doesn't God Do Something?" Garry Poole and Judson Poling, *Tough Questions: 42 Questions about God and the Bible*, special 7-in-1 edition produced for Q Place (Grand Rapids, MI: Zondervan, 2003), 237.

12. Stephen Covey, *The Seven Habits of Highly Effective People* (New York: Simon and Schuster, 1989), 237-238.

13. *Seeker Small Groups*, 143-167.

14. This excerpt is taken from *Tough Questions: 42 Questions about God and the Bible*, special 7-in-1 edition produced for Q Place, by Garry Poole & Judson Poling. Copyright © 1998, 2003 by Willow Creek Association. Used by permission of Zondervan. www.zondervan.com.

15. Cliffe Knechtle, *Give Me an Answer* (InterVarsity, 1986).

16. Marilyn Kunz and Catherine Schell, *Mark* (Q Place, 2009), 13-19.

Q PLACE RESOURCES

QUESTIONS ABOUT GOD
Tough Questions (all-in-one book)
*42 small group discussion sessions
from the entire Tough Questions series,
compiled for Q Place into one guide*
Tough Questions series
*Seven separate guides with six
discussion sessions each, available
from Q Place:*
How Does Anyone Know God Exists?
What Difference Does Jesus Make?
How Reliable Is the Bible?
How Could God Allow Suffering and Evil?
Don't All Religions Lead to God?
Do Science and the Bible Conflict?
Why Become a Christian?

BIBLE STUDY LEVEL 1
Mark – *recommended first study*
The Book of Mark *Simplified English*
Acts
Genesis
Psalms/Proverbs
Conversations with Jesus*
Lenten Studies*
Foundations for Faith*
They Met Jesus*
Suggested Level 1 starting sequences
For most groups:
Mark, Acts, Genesis
For groups that are interested in Lent:
Lenten Studies, They Met Jesus
For an overview of the Bible:
Foundations for Faith, Genesis, Mark

*Topical studies
**Character Studies

BIBLE STUDY LEVEL 2
John
Romans
Luke
1 John/James
1 Corinthians
2 Corinthians
Philippians
Colossians & Philemon
Prayer*
Change*
Treasures*
Relationships*
Servants of the Lord*
Work – God's Gift*
Celebrate*
Four Men of God**
Lifestyles of Faith, Books 1&2**

BIBLE STUDY LEVEL 3
Matthew
Galatians
1 & 2 Peter
Hebrews
1 & 2 Thessalonians,
    2 & 3 John, Jude
Isaiah
Ephesians
Set Free*
Moses**
The Life of David**

RESOURCES FOR INITIATORS
How to Start a Q Place
Seeker Small Groups
The Complete Book of Questions
Tough Questions Leader's Guide

**All resources are available through
www.QPlace.com or by calling 1-800-369-0307.**

Group Contact Information

Name	Address	Phone/Email